Reformed Church in the United States

Almanac

1879

Reformed Church in the United States

Almanac
1879

ISBN/EAN: 9783337815653

Printed in Europe, USA, Canada, Australia, Japan

Cover: Foto ©ninafisch / pixelio.de

More available books at **www.hansebooks.com**

ALMANAC

FOR

THE REFORMED CHURCH,

IN THE UNITED STATES,

FOR THE YEAR OF OUR LORD

1879.

QUESTION.—What is thy only comfort in life and death?

ANSWER.—That I, with body and soul, both in life and death, am not my own, but belong unto my faithful Saviour Jesus Christ, who, with His precious blood, hath fully satisfied for all my sins, and delivered me from all the power of the devil; and so preserves me, that, without the will of my Heavenly Father, not a hair can fall from my head; yea, that all things must be subservient to my salvation: and therefore, by His Holy Spirit, He also assures me of eternal life, and makes me sincerely willing and ready henceforth to live unto Him.

Reformed Church Publication Board,

No. 907 ARCH STREET,

PHILADELPHIA.

PUBLICATIONS OF THE REFORMED CHURCH IN THE UNITED STATES.

To be had at the following places, at the prices specified, for Cash —PHILADELPHIA, PA., Reformed Church Publication Board, 907 Arch St.
BALTIMORE, MD., John Rodenmayer, 51 Paca Street. CINCINNATI, OHIO, "Christian World," 178 Elm Street.

AT OUR PUBLICATION ROOMS, No. 907 ARCH STREET, PHILADELPHIA, ARE TO BE HAD A FULL ASSORTMENT OF

Pulpit and Family Bibles,   *Catechisms,*   *Sunday-School Books,*
Standard Theological Works,   *Hymn Books,*   *Blank Certificates,*
Miscellaneous Religious Books,   *Liturgies,*   *Stationery, &c.*

PUBLICATIONS OF THE REFORMED CHURCH.

ENGLISH AND GERMAN HYMN BOOKS

Hymns for the Reformed Church.

(NEW HYMN BOOK.)   PER COPY.

Roan Embossed, Plain	$1 00
Roan Embossed, Gilt	2 25
Imitation Turkey, Gilt	3 75
Real Turkey, Gilt	4 50
Real Turkey, Antique	4 50

Forms and Hymns

Roan Embossed, Plain	1 50
Roan Embossed, Gilt	2 50
Imitation Turkey, Gilt	4 00
Real Turkey, Gilt	5 00
Real Turkey, Antique	5 00

Order of Worship and Hymns.

Roan Embossed, Plain	2 00
Roan Embossed, Gilt	3 00
Imitation Turkey, Gilt	4 50
Real Turkey, Gilt	5 00
Real Turkey, Antique	6 00

Psalms and Hymns.

SMALL SIZE, (OLD BOOK).

Embossed Leather	75
Embossed, gilt edges	1 00
Imitation Morocco	1 50
Turkey Extra, or Antique	2 25
Turkey Extra, or Antique, with clasp	2 75
Velvet, gilt rim and clasp	7 00

LARGER SIZE. 12mo.

Plain Sheep	2 00
Roan	2 25
Roan, gilt edges	3 00
Imitation Turkey	4 00
Real Turkey, gilt or antique	4 00
Hymns and Chants for Sunday-schools bound in cloth	40
Compasion of Praise	35
German Sunday-school Hymn Book	50

Schaff's New German Hymn Book.

18mo. Embossed | 75
Embossed, gilt edges | 1 00
Imitation Morocco | 1 50
Turkey Extra or Antique | 2 50
12mo. Embossed Leather | 1 50
Embossed, gilt edges | 1 75
Imitation Morocco | 2 50
Turkey Extra or Antique | 3 50
Gesang und Choral Buch | 2 00

CATECHISMS.

Heidelberg Catechism, German or
English, embossed, with Cons. | 25
Half bound | 20
Half binding, without Cons. | 15
German and English, bound together, embossed | 50
Exercises on the Catechism | 40
Palatinate Catechism, German | 62
    "   English | 60
Catechism Simplified, paper covers | $ 12

Catechism Simplified, half binding	18
The Child's Catechism (Harbaugh's), paper	12
Half binding	18
Catechism with Proof Texts (Schaff's), half bound, per dozen	3 00
Cloth, per dozen	4 50
Catechism without Texts, half bound, per dozen	1 50
Child's Catechism, Eng. Strassburger	8
Child's Catechism or the Bible, by Rev. A. C. Whitmer	18
Paper Covers	12
Sacred Geography, with Maps, Whitmer	25
Triglott Catechism	8 50

ORDER OF WORSHIP.

Embossed leather, plain edges	1 50
" gilt edges	2 00
" red edges, with cross	2 00
Imitation morocco, full gilt	2 75
Turkey morocco or antique	4 00
Pulpit Edition, gilt or antique	7 50
Forms from the Order of Worship	40
Rev. Dr. Nevin's Answer to Dr. Dorner	25

MISCELLANEOUS.

Heaven. By Dr. Harbaugh. 12mo, clo.	1 25
Heavenly Recognition. 12mo, cloth	1 25
Heavenly Home. 12mo, cloth	1 50
Future Life. 3 vols. to match	4 00
fine edition	4 75
True Glory of Woman. Cloth	1 25
Union with the Church. Cloth	50
Life of Rev. Michael Schlatter. Cloth	1 50
Fathers of the Reformed Church. 4 vols, cloth	5 00
Golden Censer. Embossed, plain edges	1 00
Embossed, gilt edges	1 25
Imitation Turkey	1 75
Turkey or antique	2 50
Mercersburg and Modern Theology Compared. By Rev. Samuel Miller	20
The Mystical Presence. By Rev. Dr. Nevin	1 00
Creed and Customs of the Reformed Church. By Rev. O. B. Russell, D.D.	2 00
Sinai and Zion; or, a Pilgrimage Through the Wilderness to the Land of Promise. By Rev. Benjamin Bausman, D.D. With Illustrations, cloth	2 00
Fine Edition, gilt	5 00
Wayside Gleanings. By Dr. Bausman	2 00
The Voice of Blood. By Rev. S. Philips, A. M. Cloth	2 00
Philosophy and Logic. By Dr. Gerhart	1 25
Rauch's Inner Life	1 25
Wanner on the Family	75
Infant Baptism. By Dr. Bomberger	50
The Prodigal Son. By Rev. D. F. Breudle. A Practical Exposition of Luke xv. 11-32. 16mo, with Illust'ns.	1 00
The same in German	1 00
Tercentenary Monument. English	3 50
German	3 50
Salome the Dancer. Illustrated	40

Good Friday	9 42
The Ripe Harvest	50
Holy Day Stories. 8 Illustrations	50
Father Miller. 3 Illustrations	75
Life of Cain. 2 Illustrations	75
Youth in Earnest. Illustrated	90
The Old School Master. 4 Illust'ns	90
Leo Rembrandt. 4 Illustrations	90
Gospel Lessons for the Church Year. By Rev. Dr. Gans	50
Epistle Lessons for the Church Year. By Rev. Dr. Gans	50
Christological Theology. (Flexible.)	30
Easter Eggs	43
Regelien	75
Three Christmas Eves. 3 Illust'ns	1 50
Mexico	50
Alice and her Little School. 3 Illustrations	30
Harbaugh's Harfe	1 25
Constitution of the Reformed Church. Per dozen	60
Principle of Protestantism, German	50
Pennsylvania Dutch. By Prof. S. S. Haldeman. N.	1 25
Family Assistant. By Dr. S. R. Fisher. Cloth	1 25
Gift Book for the Million; or, Life Pictures of the Prodigal Son. By Rev. D. Y. Heisler, A.M.	1 00
Treasury Pictures. Vol. I.	60
Seeking and Finding	1 00
The Well Driller. By Rev. J. A. Silca.	75

CERTIFICATES.

Confirmation. Per dozen		30
" Carmine and Black		40
" Lithograph		40
Marriage. Black. Per dozen		30
" Carmine and Black		40
" Lithograph		1 50
" Photograph. Per dozen		60
Advice to Married Couples, with Marriage Certificate		60
Baptismal Certificates. German and English. Colored, per dozen		60
Extra colored, "		1 30
Gilt, "		1 15
Lithograph "		2 00
Blank Forms for Statistical Reports to Classes. Per dozen		20
Blank Calls for Special Meetings of Classes. Per dozen		30
Church Records, suitably ruled, with appropriate printed Headings for Church purposes		6 00

REWARD CARDS.

A full line of Reward Cards for Sunday Schools, and all Sunday School requisites, Class Books, Tickets, etc., etc.

SUNDAY-SCHOOL BOOKS.

The Publications of Carter & Bros., Congregational Sabbath School Society, Thos. Nelson & Sons, American Sunday-School Union, American Tract Society, Protestant Episcopal, Lutheran Publication Society, D. Lothrop & Co., and other publishers, at publishers' prices.

☞ A liberal deduction made from the above retail prices to those who buy to sell again. A copy of either of the above works will be sent by mail, postage paid, on the receipt of the retail price. The prices stated, however, are subject to the variations of the market.

SEND FOR A CATALOGUE OF SUNDAY-SCHOOL BOOKS.

ALMANAC FOR THE YEAR OF OUR LORD 1879.

Being a Common Year of 365 Days.

MOON'S SIGNS.				PLANETS AND ASPECTS.			
● New Moon.	☽ First Quarter.	● Full Moon.	☾ Last Quarter.	♄ Saturn.	♂ Mars.	♀ Venus.	☽ Moon.
				♃ Jupiter.	☉ Sun.	☿ Mercury.	♅ Herschel.

☌ Conjunction, or planets in the same longitude.   □ Quartile, when they are 90 degrees distant.
⊕ Sextile, when they are 60 degrees apart.   △ Trine, when they are 120 degrees distant.
        ☍ Opposition, when they are 180 degrees distant.

HERSCHEL'S WEATHER TABLE.

This table and the accompanying remarks are the result of many years' actual observation, the whole being constructed on a due consideration of the attraction of the Sun and Moon, in their several positions respecting the earth, and, by simple inspection, it shows the observer what kind of weather will most probably follow the entrance of the Moon into any of its quarters, and that so near the truth as to be seldom or never found to fail.

IF THE NEW MOON, FIRST QUARTER, FULL MOON OR LAST QUARTER, HAPPENS	IN SUMMER.	IN WINTER.
Between midnight and 2 o'clock	Fair	Frost unless wind Southwest.
" 2 and 4 morning	Cold and showers	Snow and stormy.
" 4 " 6 "	Rain	Rain.
" 6 " 8 "	Wind and rain	Stormy.
" 8 " 10 "	Changeable	Cold rain if wind West, snow if East.
" 10 " 12 "	Frequent showers	Cold and high wind.
" 12 " 2 afternoon	Very rainy	Snow or rain.
" 2 " 4 "	Changeable	Fair and mild.
" 4 " 6 "	Fair	Fair.
" 6 " 8 "	Fair if wind Northwest	Fair and frosty if wind N. or N. E.
" 8 " 10 "	Rainy if South or Southwest	Rain or snow if South or S. W.
" 10 " midnight	Fair	Fair and frosty.

OBSERVATIONS.—1. The nearer the time for the Moon's change, first quarter, full and last quarter are to midnight, the fairer will be the weather during the next seven days.

2. The space for this calculation occupies from ten at night till two next morning.

3. The nearer to midday or noon the phase of the Moon happens, the more foul or wet weather may be expected during the next seven days.

4. The space for this calculation occupies from ten in the forenoon to two in the afternoon. These observations refer principally to the Summer, though they affect Spring and Autumn nearly in the same ratio.

5. The Moon's change, first quarter, full and last quarter, happening during six of the afternoon hours, i. e. from four to ten, may be followed by fair weather; but this is mostly dependent on the wind, as is noted in the table.

6. Though the weather, from a variety of irregular causes, is more uncertain in the latter part of Autumn, the whole of Winter and the beginning of Spring, yet in the main the above observations will apply to those periods also.

7. To prognosticate correctly, especially in those cases where the wind is concerned, the observer should be within sight of a good vane, where the four cardinal points of the heavens are correctly placed.

CHRONOLOGICAL CYCLES.

Dominical Letter, E.   Solar Cycle, 12.   Golden Number or Lunar Cycle, 18.   Roman Indiction, 7.   Epact, 7.   Julian Period, 6592.
The Jewish Era, with their 5640th year, commences the 18th of September, 1879.
The Mohammedan Era, with their 1297th year, commences the 15th of December, 1879.

MOVEABLE FESTIVALS.

Septuagesima Sunday, Feb. 9.	Ash Wednesday, Feb. 26.	Ascension, or Holy Thurs., May 22	Corpus Christi, June 12.
Quinquagesima Sunday, Feb. 23.	Palm Sunday, April 6.	Whit Sunday, Pentecost, June 1.	First Sunday in Advent, Nov. 30.
Shrove Tuesday, Feb. 25.	Easter Sunday, April 13.	Trinity Sunday, June 8.	Sundays after Trinity are 24.

THE FOUR EMBER DAYS.

March 5.   June 4.   September 17.   December 17.

THE FOUR SEASONS OR CARDINAL POINTS.

Vernal Equinox, ☉ enters ♈ Mar. 20th, 7 o'clock, 20 min. Evening. | Autumnal Equinox, ☉ enters ♎ Sept. 23d, 5 o'clock, 12 min. Morn.
Summer Solstice, "   " ♋ June 21st, 3 " 40 " Aftern's. | Winter Solstice, "   " ♑ Dec. 21st, 10 " 14 " Eve.
       (☿) Mercury is called the Governing Planet this year.

ECLIPSES FOR THE YEAR 1879.

There will be three Eclipses, two of the Sun, and one of the Moon.

The first is an Annular Eclipse of the Sun, January 22d, 6 o'clock, 45 min. in the morning. Here invisible; visible in South America, Atlantic Ocean and Africa.

The second is an Annular Eclipse of the Sun, July 19th, 4 o'clock, 9 min. in the morning. Invisible here; visible in Europe, Africa and Indian Ocean.

The third is a partial Eclipse of the Moon, December 28th, 11 o'clock, 24 min. in the forenoon; therefore invisible here.

JANUARY, *1st Month, 31 Days.* 1879.

Weeks and Days.		Remarkable Days.	Daily Bible Lessons.	Moon R & S h. m.	Moon's Place. s.	°	Moon's Phases, Aspects of Planets, &c.	s. sl. m.	Sun rises. h. m.	Sun Sets. h. m.	High Water Phila. h. m.
Wednesday	1	*New Year*	1 Pet. 2: 12–19	12 40	♈	12	♃ sets 6 54 ◡	4	7 23	4 37	7 42
Thursday	2	Martyrs H. Scrip	Philip 2: 1–12	1 41	♈	25	☿ gr. Hel. Lat. N. ☉ in Per.	4	7 23	4 37	8 31
Friday	3	Gordius	1 Pet. 4: 12–19	2 42	♉	8	Sirius south 11 40	5	7 23	4 37	9 26
Saturday	4	Titus	Eph. 3:	3 44	♉	21	7* south 8 41	5	7 22	4 38	10 16
1] *Sunday after New Year,*			Luke 2: 33–40; Rom. 6: 12–18.				*Day's Length,* 9 *hours,* 16 *min.*				
Sunday	5	Simeon	John 1: 29–34	4 36	♊	4	☿ stationary	6	7 22	4 38	11 8
Monday	6	*Epiphany*	" 1: 38–51	5 34	♊	18	♅ rises 4 35	6	7 21	4 39	11 48
Tuesday	7	Widukind	" 2:	6 30	♋	2	♄ sets 11 8 ◠	6	7 21	4 39	12 36
Wednesday	8	Severinus	" 3:	☽ rise	♋	17	8th. Orion so. 10 31	7	7 20	4 40	1 26
Thursday	9	Catherine Zell	" 4:	6 35	♌	2	♀ in Aphelion	7	7 20	4 40	2 13
Friday	10	Paul of Thebes	" 5:	7 50	♌	17	Arctur rises 9 20 ☋	8	7 19	4 41	3 6
Saturday	11	Fructuosus	" 6: 1–25	8 57	♍	2	Spica rises 10 11	8	7 19	4 41	3 46
2] *1st Sunday after Epiphany,*			Luke 2: 41–52: Rom. 12: 1–5.				*Day's Length,* 9 *hours,* 24 *min.*				
Sunday	12	Jean Castellian	John 6: 26–71	10 10	♍	17	♃ sets 6 45	9	7 18	4 42	4 30
Monday	13	Hilary	" 7:	11 21	♎	1	Rigel south 9 27	9	7 17	4 43	5 21
Tuesday	14	Felix	" 8: 2–20	morn.	♎	15	☽ in per. Sirius so. 10 52	9	7 17	4 43	6 14
Wednesday	15	John de Laski	" 8: 21–50	12 29	♎	29	15th. ☿ rises 6 20	10	7 16	4 44	6 41
Thursday	16	Geo. Spalatine	" 9:	1 46	♏	12	☿ gr. elon. West	10	7 15	4 45	7 36
Friday	17	Anthony	" 10: 1–21	2 58	♏	25	Neptune stationary	10	7 14	4 46	8 25
Saturday	18	John Blackader	" 10: 22–42	3 38	♐	8	♄ sets 10 41	11	7 13	4 47	9 24
3] *2d Sunday after Epiphany,*			John 2: 1–11; Rom. 12: 6–16.				*Day's Length,* 9 *hours,* 36 *min.*				
Sunday	19	Heid. Cat. 1563	Mark 1: 1–20	4 37	♐	21	☌ ☽ ♅. ♅ rises 4 29	11	7 12	4 48	10 23
Monday	20	Fabian	" 1: 21–45	5 31	♑	3	☌ ☽ ☿. Pollux south 10 26 ◡	11	7 12	4 48	11 25
Tuesday	21	Agnes	" 2:	6 29	♑	15	☉ enters ♒	12	7 11	4 49	12 18
Wednesday	22	Vincent	" 3: 1–19	☽ sets	♑	27	22d. ♃ sets 6 32	12	7 10	4 50	1 16
Thursday	23	Isaiah	" 3: 20–35	6 42	♒	9	☽ ☌ ♀. ♃. ☌ ♀ ♃	12	7 9	4 51	2 4
Friday	24	Timothy	" 4:	7 38	♒	21	♀ sets 6 10 ☊	12	7 8	4 52	2 46
Saturday	25	*Paul's convers.*	" 5: 6: 1-6	8 36	♓	4	♀ in ☊. Regulus rises 6 16	13	7 7	4 53	3 29
4] *3d Sunday after Epiphany,*			Matt. 8: 1–13: Rom. 12: 17–21.				*Day's Length,* 9 *hours,* 48 *min.*				
Sunday	26	Polycarp	Mark 6: 7–29	9 38	♓	15	Spica rises 11 17	13	7 6	4 54	4 16
Monday	27	Jno. Chrysostom	" 6: 30–56	10 39	♓	27	☌ ☽ ♄. □ Neptune ☉	13	7 5	4 55	5 10
Tuesday	28	Charlemagne	" 7: 1–23	11 40	♈	9	♄ sets 10 10	13	7 4	4 56	5 42
Wednesday	29	Juventin	" 7: 24–37	morn.	♈	21	☽ in apo. Rigel so. 8 22	13	7 3	4 57	6 32
Thursday	30	Henry Müller	" 8:	12 48	♉	3	30th. ♀ sets 6 21	14	7 2	4 58	7 11
Friday	31	Hans Sachs	" 9:	1 54	♉	16	♅ rises 4 16	14	7 1	4 59	7 43

MOON'S PHASES.

Full Moon,	8th,	6 o'clock,	47 min.,	morning.
Last Quarter,	15th,	6 "	1 "	"
New Moon,	22d,	6 "	50 "	"
First Quarter,	30th,	6 "	44 "	"

CONJECTURES OF THE WEATHER.

1, 2, rain; 3, 4, 5, variable; 6, 7, cloudy, cold; 8, 9, snow; 10, 11, 12, moderate; 13, 14, 15, rain and snow; 16, N. W., cold; 17, 18, coldest days; 19, 20, moderate; 21, 22, fair; 23, cloudy; 24, 25, rain and snow; 26, 27, cold; 28, 29, snow; 30, 31, variable.

The weather is cold. Snow is on the ground. The boys are on their way to school. Their cheeks are red, and their fingers are numb, but their hearts are light. These are their happy school-days.

"HOW FRAIL I AM."

In the morning we are strong, and hardly think of weariness. So at New Year we look through all its months in hope.

And yet we have very much need to pray as did David: "Lord, make me to know .... how frail I am." (Ps. xxxix. 4.)

Our days are as an hand-breadth. Our life is but a vapor. We are short-lived as grass and flowers. Our years are few and uncertain.

Of this we should think, especially at New Year. It will make us humble, trustful, thankful and thoughtful.

CLOSED SCHOOLS.

Shutting a Sunday-school through the winter, because but few children will attend, is like saying, when through death, marriage or other removal the family has been made small,—"we will not feed these few children who are left; it is not worth while; we will break up house-keeping and let them shift for themselves!" What an idea!

"AND THE CHILD GREW."

So the Holy Ghost says of both John and Jesus. Thirty years they spent in quiet waiting and preparation for the day of their work.

From this little incident our own time and generation need to learn a great lesson,—that of a long, patient, full preparation for the work of life.

The common spirit and bad habit of our day is to hurry almost from the cradle to shop, store and desk, immature and unprepared, and thus not only unfit for work but also very liable to early decay. There is much wisdom in the old saying, "Make haste slowly."

"THE CARE OF ALL THE CHURCHES."

What was this? Not stripes, beatings, imprisonments, dangerous travel, perils by land and by sea, weariness, watchings, and daily other self-denial; but consuming "care," intense anxiety for the good of the Churches.

This every faithful minister has, not work but worry, not preaching and visitation but a daily burden of soul. He not only labors among them, but agonizes over them. This "care of all the Churches" more than anything else, takes his strength and makes gray hairs.

The slowness of some to believe, and the unfaithfulness of others, to say nothing of his own sense of weakness, his inability rightly to meet the sacred wants of his people, and the peculiar temptations of a Pastor,—weigh heavily upon his heart, giving him many a weary day and sleepless night. No wonder Paul so often said, "Brethren, pray for us."

Your Pastor tenderly bears you on his heart, in joy and sorrow, at the marriage-feast and in the house of mourning.

All this care of souls taxes his head, heart and hand to a degree which few of his people appreciate.

How, now, can you lighten this burden? How can you gladden his heart and sweeten his toil?

Thus: go to Church regularly, hear the Word gladly, live devoutly, work faithfully, pray for him daily, and give him encouraging words.

☞ We are married to Christ, that we should bring forth fruit unto God. (Rom. 7: 4.)

.5

FEBRUARY, *2d Month, 28 Days.* 1879.

Weeks and Days.		Remarkable Days.	Daily Bible Lessons.	Moon R & S h. m.	Moon's Place. s.	°	Moon's Phases, Aspects of Planets, &c.	s. sl. m.	Sun rises. h. m.	Sun sets. h. m.	High Water. Phila. h. m.
Saturday	1	Ignatius	Mark 10: 1–31	2 56		29	♀ gr. Hel. Lat. S ◡	14	6 59	5 1	8 31
5] *4th Sunday after Epiphany,*			Matt. 8: 23–37; Rom. 13: 1–7.				*Day's Length,* 10 *hours,* 4 *min.*				
Sunday	2	*Candle Mass*	Matt. 3:	3 57		13	♀ sets 6 15	14	6 58	5 2	9 29
Monday	3	Ansgar	" 4: 1–22	4 57		26	♅ rises 4 4 ⌒	14	6 57	5 3	10 24
Tuesday	4	Rhaban. Maurus	" 4:23-5:1-2.	5 50		10	☿ in Aphelion	14	6 56	5 4	11 19
Wednesday	5	P. S. Spener	" 5: 13–32	6 39		25	♄ sets 9 36 ♉	14	6 55	5 5	12 17
Thursday	6	Amandus	" 5: 32–48	☽ rise		10	6th. Sirius so. 9 17	14	6 54	5 6	1 14
Friday	7	George Wagner	" 6:	6 14		25	Orion south 8 22	14	6 53	5 7	1 54
Saturday	8	Maria Andrea	" 7:	7 32		10	☌ ♃ ⊙. Spica rises 10 20	15	6 52	5 8	2 44
6] *Septuagesima Sunday,*			Matt. 20: 1-16; 1 Cor 9: 24-27 & 10: 1-5.				*Day's Length,* 10 *hours,* 18 *min.*				
Sunday	9	John Hooper	Luke 3:	8 45		25	☽ in per. ♅ rises 5 56	15	6 51	5 9	3 30
Monday	10	F. C. Oetinger	" 4:	9 59		10	♄ sets 9 20	15	6 49	5 11	4 19
Tuesday	11	H. de St. Victor	" 5:	11 15		25	Arctur rises 9 18	15	6 48	5 12	5 14
Wednesday	12	Lady Jane Grey	" 6: 1–19	morn.		9	♀ sets 6 24	15	6 47	5 13	6 6
Thursday	13	C. F. Schwartz	" 6: 20–49	12 30		22	13th. Aldebaran south 6 42	15	6 46	5 14	6 44
Friday	14	Brun. of Querfu't	" 7:	1 38		5	Orion south 7 55	14	6 44	5 16	7 32
Saturday	15	Jacob von Loh	" 8:	2 38		18	Andromeda sets 9 55	14	6 43	5 17	8 26
7] *Sexagesima Sunday,*			Luke 8: 4-15; 2 Cor. 11: 19-33 & 12: 1-9.				*Day's Length,* 10 *hours,* 36 *min.*				
Sunday	16	Matth. Desübas	Luke 9: 1–36	3 32		1	☌ ☽ ♅. ♅ rises 3 49 ◡	14	6 42	5 18	9 22
Monday	17	Pat. Hamilton	" 9: 37–62	4 15		13	♄ sets 8 38	14	6 40	5 20	10 19
Tuesday	18	Simeon of Jerus.	" 10:	5 14		25	7* sets 1 2	14	6 39	5 21	11 17
Wednesday	19	Mesrob	" 11:	5 56		7	☊. ⊙ enters ♓	14	6 38	5 22	12 16
Thursday	20	Sadoth	" 11:37-12:1-12	☽ sets		19	20th. ☽ ☌ ♃. ☿	14	6 37	5 23	1 19
Friday	21	Mainrod	" 12: 13–59	6 30		1	Capella south 6 48	14	6 36	5 24	1 57
Saturday	22	*Washington B.*	" 13: 1–21	7 27		12	☌ ☽ ♀. ♀ sets 6 51	14	6 34	5 26	2 42
8] *Quinquagesima Sunday,*			Luke 18: 31–43; 1 Cor. 13: 1–43.				*Day's Length,* 10 *hours,* 54 *min.*				
Sunday	23	B. Ziegenbalg	Luke 13: 22–35	8 26		24	☌ ☽ ♄. ♄ sets 8 20	14	6 33	5 27	3 30
Monday	24	Matthias	" 14:	9 24		6	Sirius south 8 11	13	6 32	5 28	4 12
Tuesday	25	*Shrove Tuesday*	" 15:	10 26		22	☽ in apo. ☿ gr. Hel. Lat. S.	13	6 31	5 29	4 51
Wednesday	26	*Ash Wednesday*	" 16:	11 30		10	♅ rises 3 30	13	6 29	5 31	5 40
Thursday	27	Martin Bucer	" 17: 1–19	morn.		25	Antares rises 2 10	13	6 28	5 32	6 20
Friday	28	Jno. de Mon. Corv.	" 17: 20–37	12 42		8	Regulus rises 11 2	13	6 27	5 33	6 59

MOON'S PHASES.

Full Moon,	6th,	8 o'clock,	42 min.,	evening.
Last Quarter,	13th,	1 "	55 "	afternoon.
New Moon,	20th,	11 "	3 "	evening.

CONJECTURES OF THE WEATHER.

1, 2, fair; 3, 4, cloudy, snow; 5, 6, cold, N. W.; 7, 8, snow; 9, 10, 11, variable; 12, 13, 14, cold; 15, 16, moderate; 17, 18, 19, variable; 20, 21, 22, fair; 23, 24, snow; 25, 26, variable; 27, 28, fair.

(♀.) Venus is Evening Star till September 23d. Then Morning Star till the end of the year.

(♃.) Jupiter is in conjunction with the Sun the 8th of this month, and cannot be seen.

Every American child should know the face of the great and good WASHINGTON, and know also much of his early and later history. The boy that honored his mother led the Colonial Army to victory.

LENT.

Lent is the special penitential season of six weeks before Easter to prepare for the solemnities of Good Friday and the joys of Easter.

Ash Wednesday, the first day of Lent, is so called from the old Jewish and early Christian custom of throwing ashes upon the head as a token of sorrow and repentance (Esther iv. 3; Dan. ix. 3; Matt. xi. 21).

Count from Ash Wednesday to Easter, and you have forty-six days; but as the Lord's Day can never be a day of fasting and sorrow, but only of rejoicing in remembrance of Christ's resurrection, the six Sundays in Lent must be counted out, and you have a season of forty days, in commemoration, especially, of the Saviour's forty days' fasting and praying in the wilderness (Matt. iv. 1–11).

Fasting with us is optional, of course; but is it well to neglect it? Examine the Old Testament, yes, and also the New Testament, and you may be surprised to see how much is said about this divinely appointed form of worship. It need not, indeed must not, be a mere bodily exercise profiting little. Fasting is optional; but confession of sin, self-examination, and humiliation of soul, are not optional.

During the Lenten season, let us devoutly turn our hearts and minds toward the suffering Saviour, and meditate on His holy love and great humiliation, as well as upon our sins.

STRIFE AND DIVISIONS IN THE CHURCH.

1). *They are very old.* Paul and Barnabas had a sharp contention (Acts xv. 39). Paul and Peter had a warm debate at Antioch (Gal. ii. 11). The congregation at Corinth had four parties (1 Cor. i. 10–12). It is not strange, then, that in every age the Church has had strife and division. And it is safe to say that these will continue down to the second coming of Christ.

2). *They are the conflict* between grace and sin, between truth and error, and are some sign of a living Church struggling against the power of evil. Truth must oppose error, and error will persecute truth. And it is simply astonishing to see in how many ways the devil manages to bring about the most unfortunate differences, which then must be met by the positive power of the Holy Ghost.

3). *They are always over-ruled for good.* If Rom. viii. 28 is true of the individual, how much more so of His Church as a whole! The very heresies of the early Church brought out all those rich apologetic writings of the Fathers. What a wealth of Scriptural learning the Reformation developed! So to-day infidelity, Romanism, and denominational questions have given us vast stores of valuable Christian literature.

And yet, of course, while divine wisdom over-rules all these follies and evils, divisions and contentions, for the good of His Church, nevertheless they are to be lamented, yea, first of all to be avoided if possible. God makes even the wrath of man to serve Him, but no thanks to man.

4). Amid all these troubles, *we must never lose confidence in the Church.* The Church, as once her Lord, is now in her state of humiliation, and her glory is hid; but at His second Coming she will shine forth in beauty. The Church militant cannot be at peace till the warfare is over. Till then, we must wait, and pray and work for her peace and prosperity, sure of her victory.

COSTLY WORSHIP.

Many city churches pay immense sums for their music. In New York and Boston a first-class quartette, with organist, costs from $6,000 to $12,000 a year. Good singers are well paid, from $1,000 to $7,000. Such worship, too, is often more costly than devout.

MARCH, *3d Month, 31 Days.* 1879.

Weeks and Days.		Remarkable Days.	Daily Bible Lessons.	Moon R & S h. m.	Moon's Place. s. a.	Moon's Phases, Aspects of Planets, &c.	s. sl. m.	Sun rises. h. m.	Sun Sets. h. m.	High Water Phila. h. m.
Saturday	1	Suidbert	Luke 18: 1–30	1 40	♍ 21	☽ 1st. ☌ ♀ ♄. ♄ [illegible] ⌣	13	6 25	5 35	7 40
9] *1st Sunday in Lent,*			Matt. 4: 1–11; 2 Cor. 6: 1–10.			*Day's Length,* 11 *hours,* 12 *min.*				
Sunday	2	John Wesley	Luke 16: 31–19: 1–28	2 36	♎ 5	♀ sets 7 8 ⌢	13	6 24	5 36	8 29
Monday	3	Bathilde	" 19: 29–20: 1–18	3 30	♎ 19	♅ rises 8 22	12	6 23	5 37	9 14
Tuesday	4	Geo. Wishart	" 20: 19–21: 1–4	4 21	♏ 3	☌ ☿ ☉ Superior	12	6 21	5 39	10 4
Wednesday	5	*Emberday*	" 21: 5–35	4 54	♏ 18	Sirius south 7 34	12	6 20	5 40	10 42
Thursday	6	Fridolin	" 22: 1–30	5 29	♐ 3	☋. Spica rises 8 44	11	6 19	5 41	11 30
Friday	7	Perpetua	" 22: 31–71	5 59	♐ 18	Castor south 8 13	11	6 17	5 43	12 26
Saturday	8	Zach. Ursinus	" 23:	☽ rise	♑ 4	8th. Arctur rises 7 42	11	6 16	5 44	1 20
10] *2d Sunday in Lent,*			Matt. 15: 21–28; 1 Thes. 4: 1–8.			*Day's Length,* 11 *hours,* 30 *min.*				
Sunday	9	Cyrillus	Mark 10: 32–52	7 36	♑ 19	☽ in per. ♀ sets 7 42	11	6 15	5 45	2 10
Monday	10	40 Martyrs at Sebaste	" 11:	8 39	♒ 3	♅ rises 8 8	10	6 13	5 47	2 50
Tuesday	11	Wm. Hoseus	" 12:	9 40	♒ 17	♄ sets 7 42	10	6 12	5 48	3 41
Wednesday	12	Greg. the Great	" 13:	10 46	♓ 1	Regulus south 10 30	10	6 11	5 49	4 31
Thursday	13	Rudericus	" 14: 1–54	11 50	♓ 15	Wega rises 10 19	10	6 10	5 50	5 20
Friday	14	Matilda	" 14: 55–15: 1–15	morn.	♓ 28	14th. Orion sets 12 34 ⌣	9	6 8	5 52	6 15
Saturday	15	Thos. Cranmer	" 15: 16–47	12 52	♈ 10	7* sets 11 27	9	6 7	5 53	7 10
11] *3d Sunday in Lent,*			Luke 11: 14–28; Eph. 5: 1–9.			*Day's Length,* 11 *hours,* 50 *min.*				
Sunday	16	Heribert	Matt. 20: 17–33	1 46	♈ 22	♄ sets 7 26	9	6 5	5 55	7 43
Monday	17	St. Patrick	" 21:	2 30	♉ 4	☌ ☽ ♅. ♅ rises 2 51	8	6 4	5 56	8 32
Tuesday	18	Alexander	" 22:	3 10	♉ 16	♀ sets 7 40	8	6 3	5 57	9 21
Wednesday	19	Mary & Martha	" 23:	3 50	♉ 28	☊. ♃ rises 4 24 Mor.	8	6 2	5 58	10 19
Thursday	20	Ambrose of Sien	" 24: 1–31	4 32	♊ 9	☌ ☽ ♃. ☉ enters ♈. D. & N. equal.	8	6 0	6 0	11 18
Friday	21	Benedict	" 24: 31–51	5 12	♊ 21	Spring commences	7	5 59	6 1	12 16
Saturday	22	Nich v. d. Flüe	" 25:	☽ sets	♋ 3	22d. Sirius sets 11 34	7	5 57	6 3	1 16
12] *4th Sunday in Lent,*			John 6: 1–14; Gal. 4: 21–31.			*Day's Length,* 12 *hours,* 8 *min.*				
Sunday	23	Wolfgang	Matt. 26: 1–13	7 25	♋ 15	☌ ☽ ♄. ♄ sets 7 10	7	5 56	6 4	1 44
Monday	24	Florentius	Mark 26: 14–35	8 15	♋ 27	☌ ☽ ☿. ♅ rises 2 30	6	5 54	6 6	2 35
Tuesday	25	Ann. V. Mary	" 26: 36–56	9 10	♌ 9	☽ in apo. ☌ ☽ ♀. 8 20	6	5 53	6 7	3 28
Wednesday	26	Lindger	" 26: 57; 27: 1–2	10 26	♌ 22	☌ ☽ ☉. ♀ sets	6	5 52	6 8	4 14
Thursday	27	Rupertus	" 27: 3–31	11 39	♍ 5	♃ rises 4 4	5	5 51	6 9	5 11
Friday	28	John von Goch	" 27: 32–50	morn.	♍ 18	☿ sets 7 2	5	5 49	6 11	5 55
Saturday	29	Eustatius	" 27: 51–56	12 37	♎ 1	☿ gr. elong. East ⌢	5	5 48	6 12	6 40
13] *5th Sunday in Lent,*			John 8: 46–59; Heb. 9: 11–15.			*Day's Length,* 12 *hours,* 26 *min.*				
Sunday	30	John Heermann	John 11:	1 41	♎ 14	30th. ♀ in ☊	4	5 47	6 13	7 31
Monday	31	Ernest the Pious	" 12:	2 27	♎ 28	☿ gr. Hel. Lat. N.	4	5 45	6 15	8 24

MOON'S PHASES.

First Quarter,	1st,	2 o'clock,	58 min.,	morning.	
Full Moon,	8th,	8 "	9 "	"	
Last Quarter,	14th,	10 "	42 "	evening.	
New Moon,	22d,	4 "	0 "	afternoon.	
First Quarter,	30th,	8 "	6 "	evening.	

CONJECTURES OF THE WEATHER.

1, 2, snow; 3, 4, 5, clear, cold; 6, variable; 7, 8, rain and snow; 9, 10, 11, N. W., cold; 12, 13, 14, fair; 15, 16, variable; 17, 18, rain; 19, 20, 21, clear; 22, 23, showers; 24, 25, rain; 26, 27, 28, fair; 29, cloudy; 30, 31, clear.

(♄.) Saturn is in conjunction with the Sun the 26th of this month, and cannot be seen.

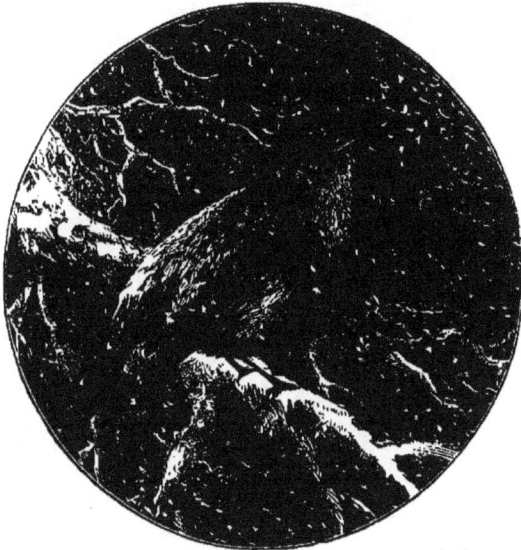

"Glad to see you, little bird,
'Twas your little chirp I heard;
What did you intend to say?
'Give me something this cold day?'"

"That I will, and plenty too;
All the crumbs I saved for you:
Don't be frightened—here's a treat:
I will wait and see you eat."

FORBEARING.

To bear a wrong is often much easier than to have it made right.

When people say or do what wounds you, of course you may call them to account, make great ado, demand apology, and all that; but is it best?

A much better plan generally, is to bear tho wrong. Our old nature says: "Pay him back in his own coin," but the Spirit says: "Forbearing one another in love."

This bearing a wrong with patience is good for self, because it is a victory over evil; and it is good also for those who wrong us, for love always wins.

"THOU ART THE MAN."

All men groan under sin, and make some outcry for mercy. True penitence, humiliation, confession and peace are possible, however, only under Christianity, and in the Christian Church.

To cloak or hide our sin, to excuse or justify it, is great folly. Much less may we get angry at the servant of the Lord for rebuking it. Like the royal sinner of Israel we must cry, "Have mercy upon me, O God, according to thy loving-kindness."

In repentance, much depends on how we look at our sins, whether as against man, or as against God. As God is higher than man, so will our contrition be deeper if we look upon sin (as David did, Ps. li. 4) as against God our loving Heavenly Father.

True repentance is not just occasional, spasmodic and passing, but abiding. Nor will it fail to make prompt and hearty confession, saying, "I have sinned."

And we need to look away from sinful self to Him who alone can take away our sin. We need not only pardon but cleansing; not only peace but purity; not only the washing of regeneration, but also the renewing of the Holy Ghost.

WHY MUST WE TEACH CHILDREN?

(1.) Because God has given them brains. Created in His image, they need to know all they can about the word and works of God. Some children do not even know that they have souls, much less that they are sinners and need redemption. All this knowledge must be given them, as truly as you have received all that you know. It will not come to them of itself.

(2.) Because of the infidelity around them. Many false views prevail. The devil is busy sowing error. Our children must be made able to meet and overcome all these forms of unbelief. Nothing can so well fit them for this as careful instruction in the truth of God. Knowledge and grace go together.

9

Weeks and Days.		Remarkable Days.	Daily Bible Lessons.	Moon R & S h. m.	Moon's Place. s. a.	Moon's Phases, Aspects of Planets, &c.	s. sl. m.	Sun rises. h. m.	Sun sets. h. m.	High Water Phila. h. m.
Tuesday	1	Fritigiid	John 13: 1–30	2 56	12	☋. ♀ sets 8 22 ⌒	4	5 44	6 16	9 12
Wednesday	2	Theodosia	" 13: 31–14	3 24	27	♅ rises 2 23	4	5 43	6 17	9 48
Thursday	3	Gerh. Tersteegen	" 15:	4 0	12	♃ rises 3 34	3	5 41	6 19	10 36
Friday	4	Ambrose	" 16:	4 30	27	Sirius sets 10 47	3	5 40	6 20	11 24
Saturday	5	Christ. Scriver	" 17:	4 59	12	Orion sets 11 20	3	5 39	6 21	12 19
14] *Palm Sunday,*			John 12: 1–16; Phil. 2: 5–11.			*Day's Length,* 12 *hours,* 44 *min.*				
Sunday	6	Albert Durer	Lam. Jeremiah	☽ rise	27	6th. Regulus [illegible]	2	5 38	6 22	1 16
Monday	7	Olaus Peterson	Heb. 8:	7 48	11	☽ in per. ☿ station.	2	5 37	6 23	1 54
Tuesday	8	Mart. Chemnitz.	" 9:	9 4	25	7* sets 10 2	2	5 35	6 25	2 41
Wednesday	9	Thos. v. Westen	" 10:	10 18	9	♀ sets 8 45	2	5 34	6 26	3 13
Thursday	10	*Maund. Thurs.*	John 6:	11 24	23	♅ rises 2 12	1	5 33	6 27	4 32
Friday	11	*Good Friday*	Luke 23: 32–49	morn.	6	♃ rises 3 14 ◡	1	5 31	6 29	5 20
Saturday	12	Sabas	Heb. 4:	12 18	18	Wega rises 8 56	1	5 30	6 30	5 54
15] *Easter Sunday,*			John 20: 1–10; Col. 3: 1–11.			*Day's Length,* 13 *hours,* 2 *min.*				
Sunday	13	*Easter Sunday*	John 20: 1–18	12 52	0	13th. Antares [illegible]	0	5 29	6 31	6 42
Monday	14	*Easter Monday*	Luke 24: 1–12	1 28	13	Rigel sets 10 5	Sun	5 28	6 32	7 31
Tuesday	15	Simon Dach	Acts 2: 22–47	1 56	24	☌ ☽ ♅. ♅ rises 2 1	fast	5 27	6 33	8 26
Wednesday	16	Peter Waldo	1 Cor. 15:	2 22	6	☊. ☌ ☽ ♃. ♃ rises 2 41	0	5 26	6 34	9 13
Thursday	17	Mappalicus	Rom. 6:	2 49	17	☌ ☿ ☉ Inferior	1	5 24	6 36	9 46
Friday	18	Luther at Worms	" 8:	3 12	29	♀ sets 9 18	1	5 23	6 37	10 38
Saturday	19	Melancthon	1 Cor. 3:	3 40	11	☌ ☽ ♄. ♄ rises 3 58	1	5 21	6 39	11 30
16] *1st Sunday after Easter,*			John 20: 19–31; 1 John 5: 4–10.			*Day's Length,* 13 *hours,* 20 *min.*				
Sunday	20	John Bugenhag	John 1:	4 12	23	☌ ☽ ☿. ☉ ent. ♉	2	5 20	6 40	12 28
Monday	21	Anselm of Cant.	" 2:	☽ sets	6	21st. ☽ in apo.	2	5 19	6 41	1 24
Tuesday	22	Origen	" 3:	8 30	19	Sirius sets 9 40	2	5 18	6 42	2 12
Wednesday	23	Adelbert	" 4:	9 31	2	Orion sets 10 6	2	5 17	6 43	3 4
Thursday	24	Wilfrid	" 5:	10 20	15	☌ ☽ ♀. ♀ sets 9 30	2	5 15	6 45	3 42
Friday	25	St. Mark, Evan.	" 6: 1–10	11 24	26	7* sets 8 55 ⌒	2	5 14	6 46	4 30
Saturday	26	Trudpert	" 6: 41–71	morn.	11	♃ rises 2 11	3	5 13	6 47	5 15
17] *2d Sunday after Easter,*			John 10: 11–16; 1 Pet. 2: 20–25.			*Day's Length,* 13 *hours,* 36 *min.*				
Sunday	27	Otto Catelin	John 7:	12 20	25	♅ rises 1 54	3	5 12	6 48	5 50
Monday	28	Fred. Myconius	" 8: 1–30	1 10	9	♄ rises 3 39	3	5 11	6 49	6 41
Tuesday	29	L. von Berquin	" 8: 31–59	1 59	23	29th. ☿ stationary	3	5 10	6 50	7 32
Wednesday	30	Geo. Calixtus	" 9:	2 28	7	☋. ☌ Neptune ☉	3	5 9	6 51	8 20

MOON'S PHASES.

Full Moon,	6th,	5 o'clock,	24 min.	evening.
Last Quarter,	13th,	9 "	9 "	morning.
New Moon,	21st,	8 "	55 "	"
First Quarter,	29th,	9 "	16 "	"

CONJECTURES OF THE WEATHER.

1, 2, 3, fair; 4, 5, stormy; 6, 7, rain; 8, 9, 10, fair; 11, 12, variable; 13, 14, showers; 15, 16, 17, fair; 18, 19, variable; 20, 21, thunder showers; 22, 23, fair; 24, 25, 26, rain; 27, 28, 29, variable; 30, fair.

Making up after a quarrel is not so easy as to keep from quarreling; but it is a noble and wise thing to do. Never be afraid or ashamed to confess a wrong. Never wait long for another " to speak first."

"THE LORD IS RISEN INDEED."

Easter joy is only for the Christian. To the natural man it is foolishness, because he cannot discern it. To him the Easter song is an empty sound, and our joy is an idle tale. This is true of Easter as it is true, and especially because it is true, of all the things of the Spirit of God. He receiveth them not, because they are spiritually discerned.

"WOUNDED FOR OUR TRANSGRESSIONS."

"Sinful soul, what hast thou done ?
Crucified God's only Son."

In thinking of the death of our blessed Saviour every one should confess his own share of the curse that rested on Him. Only so can we share the benefit of His redeeming work.

WHAT THE CONSTITUTION SAYS.

No one can be ordained to the Holy Ministry under twenty-one years of age.

A Minister is bound to continue in the service of the sanctuary as long as he lives; nor dare he devote himself to any secular calling, at his own pleasure.

Members of the Church must, by a proper support, place their Ministers above disturbing want, that they may give themselves entirely to their sacred work.

Our Church Courts are these: Consistory, Classis, Synod, and General Synod. The last meets only every three years.

Each Synod shall give every necessary attention to the education of poor young men for the Ministry, and to both Home Missions and Foreign Missions, as well as to the publication of books and papers for the Church.

"All baptized persons are members of the Church, under its care, and subject to its government and discipline."

"A child may be baptized, if one of the parents be a communicant member; but if neither of them be such, it must remain for the present unbaptized, agreeably to 1 Cor. vii. 14."

Baptisms should be in the Church, and parents must themselves take every vow.

Every Minister shall give special attention to the instruction of the young to prepare them for full membership. The Elders shall be present, if possible, at this catechization.

Persons become full members of the Church by the rite of confirmation.

Members removing shall obtain a certificate of dismission, and connect themselves at the earliest opportunity with the congregation to whose bounds they have removed. This certificate is good for only one year.

No Minister shall accept payment for administering Baptism or the Lord's Supper and so make traffic of sacred things. The same ought to hold also in regard to funerals, says the Constitution. He should have a proper salary, and all his services should then be free.

Family worship and prayer-meetings during the week are important. ____

☞ Bear ye one another's burdens, burdens of work and of weakness, of joy and of sorrow. This is the love and the law of Christ.

MAY, *5th Month, 31 Days.* 1879.

Weeks and Days.		Remarkable Days.	Daily Bible Lessons.	Moon R & S h. m.	Moon's Place s. a.	Moon's Phases, Aspects of Planets, &c.	s. fs. m.	Sun rises. h. m.	Sun Sets. h. m.	High Water. Phila. h. m.
Thursday	1	Philip & James	John 10:	2 50	22	♀ sets 9 38 ⌒	3	5 7	6 53	9 11
Friday	2	Athanasius	" 11:	3 10	7	♀ in Perihelion	3	5 6	6 54	9 51
Saturday	3	Monica	" 12:	3 35	22	☿ in Aphelion	3	5 5	6 55	10 42
18]		*3d Sunday after Easter,*	John 16: 16–22; 1 Pet. 2: 11–19.			*Day's Length*, 13 *hours*, 52 *min.*				
Sunday	4	Florian	John 13: 14:	3 55	6	⛢ rises 1 48	3	5 4	6 56	11 36
Monday	5	Fred. the Wise	" 15:	4 20	20	☽ in per. ♄ rises 3 19	3	5 3	6 57	12 32
Tuesday	6	John of Damasc.	" 16: 17:	☽ rise	4	○ 6th. 7* sets 8 24	3	5 2	6 58	1 30
Wednesday	7	Otto the Great	" 18:	9 14	18	Spica south 10 20	4	5 1	6 59	2 22
Thursday	8	Stanislaus	" 19:	10 16	1	♅ stationary ⌣	4	5 0	7 0	3 10
Friday	9	Gr'g. Nanzianzen	" 20:	11 4	15	☌ ⛢ ♃. ♃ rises 1 10	4	4 59	7 1	4 6
Saturday	10	John Heuglin	" 21:	11 46	26	♀ sets 9 50	4	4 58	7 2	4 41
19]		*4th Sunday after Easter,*	John 16: 5–15: James 1: 16–21.			*Day's Length*, 14 *hours*, 6 *min.*				
Sunday	11	John Arndt	Heb. 1: 2:	morn.	8	♄ rises 2 54 ☊	4	4 57	7 3	5 32
Monday	12	Meletius	" 3: 4:	12 20	20	☾ 12. Orion sets 8 56	4	4 56	7 4	6 24
Tuesday	13	Servatius	" 5: 6:	12 49	2	⛢ rises 1 39	4	4 55	7 5	7 10
Wednesday	14	Pachomius	" 7:	1 16	14	☽ ♀ ♃. ⛢. ☿ gr. elong. W.	4	4 54	7 6	8 5
Thursday	15	Moses	" 8:	1 39	26	☿ rises 3 55	4	4 53	7 7	8 42
Friday	16	Martyrs at L.	" 9:	2 2	8	♃ rises 1 0	4	4 52	7 8	9 32
Saturday	17	Joachim of Flor.	" 10:	2 25	21	☌ ☽ ♄. ♄ rises 2 30	4	4 51	7 9	10 20
20]		*5th Sunday after Easter,*	John 16: 23–33; James 1: 22–27.			*Day's Length*, 14 *hours*, 20 *min.*				
Sunday	18	80 Marts. under Val.	Heb. 11:	2 50	2	☽ in apo. ♀ sets 10 0	4	4 50	7 10	11 14
Monday	19	Alcuin	" 12:	3 20	15	☌ ☽ ☿. Sirius sets 7 56	4	4 50	7 10	11 54
Tuesday	20	Val. Herberger	" 13:	3 49	28	Arctur south 10 20	4	4 49	7 11	12 38
Wednesday	21	Constantine	John 14:	☽ sets	11	● 21. □ ⛢ ☉. ☉ ent. ♊	4	4 48	7 12	1 28
Thursday	22	*Ascension Day*	Col. 2:	8 59	24	♃ rises 12 46 ⌒	4	4 47	7 13	2 20
Friday	23	Jerome Savanor.	John 15:	9 54	8	⛢ rises 1 22	4	4 46	7 14	3 16
Saturday	24	Augustine Cazal	" 16:	10 39	22	♀ gr. Hel. Lat. N. ☌ ☽ ♀	3	4 46	7 14	4 8
21]		*6th Sunday after Easter,*	John 15: 26; 16: 1; 1 Pet. 4: 7–11.			*Day's Length*, 14 *hours*, 30 *min.*				
Sunday	25	Augustine	1 John 1:	11 27	6	♀ sets 10 12 ☋	3	4 45	7 15	4 46
Monday	26	Beda Venerabilis	" 2:	11 59	20	♄ rises 2 0	3	4 44	7 16	5 30
Tuesday	27	John Calvin	" 3:	morn.	4	Orion sets 7 18	3	4 43	7 17	6 15
Wednesday	28	Lanfranc	" 4:	12 46	18	☽ 28th. Arctur south 9 48	3	4 43	7 17	6 54
Thursday	29	David Zeisberger	" 5:	1 10	2	Regulus sets 12 21	3	4 42	7 18	7 42
Friday	30	Jer'me of Prague	Joel 3:	1 39	16	Pollux sets 10 56	3	4 41	7 19	8 31
Saturday	31	Joac'm Neander	John 17:	2 6	0	♃ rises 12 20	3	4 41	7 19	9 23

MOON'S PHASES.

Full Moon,	6th,	1 o'clock,	11 min.,	morning.
Last Quarter,	12th,	9 "	35 "	evening.
New Moon,	21st,	12 "	50 "	morning.
First Quarter,	28th,	6 "	36 "	evening.

CONJECTURES OF THE WEATHER.

1, 2, thunder showers; 3, 4, cloudy; 5, cool; 6, 7, 8, warm; 9, 10, cloudy; 11, showers; 12, 13, 14, fair; 15, 16, showers; 17, 18, 19, variable; 20, 21, fair; 22, 23, rain; 24, 25, 26, fair; 27, 28, warm; 29, 30, showers; 31, fair.

This boy has a good motto on his banner. *Excelsior* is a Latin word and means "higher yet." So all should say: boys about their lessons, men about their work, and Christians in regard to a godly life. Some people are too lazy, and others are too careless, to rise either in business or goodness.

"HE ASCENDED INTO HEAVEN."

"Ever upward let us move,
Wafted on the wings of love,
Looking when our Lord shall come,
Looking for a happier home."

The Ascension of Christ has brought heaven very near, and made it very real. It now is our Father's house, a place of rest, a better country, the true Canaan.

WHEN TO GO TO CHURCH.

The parents of Jesus went regularly, (Luke ii. 41), and so some faithful souls now do; but many people go only when they feel like it,—that is, when the sky is clear, and the air not too hot, nor yet too cold, when they have no toothache, nor any visitors, in other words, when everything is favorable, and when convenience is at its height. What a sickly Christianity that is! Away with it! Go to church when the time comes.

☞ Some persons think that their vows rest upon them only so long as their name is in the Church book; but they forget that God holds us to our vows *forever*.

EDUCATIONAL RELIGION.

Our baptized children are "in the Lord," and therefore to be brought up in His "nurture and admonition."

This is "Educational" religion, and is merely the fulfilment of the baptismal vows which bind the parents and congregation to train and teach the child in the way of godliness. The grace of God at hand in the child, makes this nurture and admonition possible.

To our baptized children we say: "You are holy unto the Lord and stand in His favor; throw not away this glory but cherish your heirship. You by nature are a poor sinner, but Christ has made you His own; love Him for His love, and live to His praise. God is your Father; live as His holy child. The Holy Ghost is given you to comfort you and abide with you forever; yield yourself always to His gracious in-working."

Nor do we wrong our children, when we thus bias them toward goodness. Were Samuel and Timothy wronged by being from childhood under the nurture and admonition of the Lord? Was it not Abraham's praise that he commanded his children after him? The child, while yet a child, shall be trained up in the way he should go.

NOTES ON THE HEIDELBERG CATECHISM.

This new work of three hundred and twenty-three pages, has lately been published by Rev. A. C. Whitmer of Altoona, Pa. Price, bound in cloth, one dollar per copy, to be had of the author, or from the Reformed Church Publication Board.

These *Notes* are not sermons, but a simple and concise explanation of the text of the Catechism, and will be found very valuable for parents, teachers and catechumens. They contain much important instruction, brought within small compass, and are very suggestive. A detailed alphabetical index at the close is also worth mentioning.

As we have so little in English on the Catechism, in a form to be easily put into the hands of our young people, this work should meet a great want, and be widely circulated.

The book is neatly gotten up, well bound, and is sold at a very low price.

☞ Every Christian has his crosses, and these crosses are as different as faces.

JUNE, *6th Month, 30 Days.* 1879.

Weeks and Days.		Remarkable Days.	Daily Bible Lessons.	Moon R & S h. m.	Moon's Place. s. a.	Moon's Phases, Aspects of Planets, &c.	s. fs. m.	Sun rises. h. m.	Sun sets. h. m.	High Water. Phila. h. m.
22] *Whit Sunday or Pentecost,*			John 14: 15–31; Act 2: 1–11.			*Day's Length,* 14 *hours,* 40 *min.*				
Sunday	1	*Whit Sunday*	Gal. 3: 4: 1–7	2 32	♏ 14	♀ sets 10 21 ⌒	3	4 40	7 20	10 24
Monday	2	*Whit Monday*	" 5:	2 54	♏ 28	□ ♃ ☉. ♅ rises 1 3	2	4 40	7 20	11 23
Tuesday	3	Chlotilde	Romans 12:	3 18	♐ 12	☽ in per. ♄ rises 1 31	2	4 39	7 21	12 23
Wednesday	4	*Emberday*	1 Cor. 13:	☽ rise	♐ 26	4th. ♃ rises 12 10 ◡	2	4 39	7 21	1 22
Thursday	5	Boniface	Rom. 6: 19–7:	9 0	♑ 9	Spica south 8 25	2	4 38	7 22	2 18
Friday	6	Norbert	" 8:	9 46	♑ 21	Antares south 11 18	2	4 38	7 22	3 8
Saturday	7	Paul Gerhart	2 Cor. 5:	10 20	♒ 4	Altair south 12 42	2	4 38	7 22	3 46
23] *Trinity Sunday,*			John 3: 1–15; Rev. 4: 1–11.			*Day's Length,* 14 *hours,* 46 *min.*				
Sunday	8	A. H. Francke	Acts 1: 2:	10 50	♒ 16	☊. ♀ sets 10 22	1	4 37	7 23	4 34
Monday	9	Columba	" 3:	11 18	♒ 28	Procyon sets 8 42	1	4 37	7 23	5 20
Tuesday	10	Fred. Barbarossa	" 4:	11 45	♓ 10	Regulus sets 11 29	1	4 37	7 23	6 10
Wednesday	11	Barnabas	" 5:	morn.	♓ 22	11. ☌ ☽ ♃. ♃ rises 11 55	1	4 36	7 24	6 46
Thursday	12	Renata	" 6:	12 10	♈ 4	☌ ☽ ♅. ♅ rises 12 40	1	4 36	7 24	7 31
Friday	13	Isaac Le Febre	" 7:	12 34	♈ 16	☌ ☽ ♄. ♄ rises 1 2	1	4 36	7 24	8 21
Saturday	14	Basil	" 8:	1 1	♈ 28	Libræ south 9 10	sun	4 35	7 25	9 12
24] *1st Sunday after Trinity,*			Luke 16: 19–21; John 4: 7–20.			*Day's Length,* 14 *hours,* 50 *min.*				
Sunday	15	W. Wilberforce	1 Pet. 2: 1–10	1 29	♉ 10	☽ in apo. ♅ gr. Hel. Lat. S.	slow	4 35	7 25	9 46
Monday	16	Richard Baxter	Acts 10:	2 2	♉ 23	☿ in Perihelion	1	4 35	7 25	10 40
Tuesday	17	John Tauler	" 11:	2 43	♊ 6	♀ sets 10 17	1	4 35	7 25	11 34
Wednesday	18	Pamphilus	" 12:	3 34	♊ 20	☌ ☿ ☉ Superior	1	4 35	7 25	12 24
Thursday	19	Council at Nice	1 Pet. 2: 11-3: 1-17	☽ sets	♋ 3	19. ☌ ☽ ☿. ♃ rises 11 .. ⌒	1	4 35	7 25	1 14
Friday	20	27 Martyrs	" 3: 18-4: 16	8 46	♋ 17	♄ rises 12 46	1	4 35	7 25	1 58
Saturday	21	Matth. Claudius	" 4: 17-5:	9 20	♌ 1	☉ ent. ♋. Longest Day	2	4 34	7 26	2 42
25] *2d Sunday after Trinity,*			Luke 14: 16–24; 1 John 3: 13–21.			*Day's Length,* 14 *hours,* 50 *min.*				
Sunday	22	Gottschalk	James 1:	10 1	♌ 15	☋. Summer com.	2	4 35	7 25	3 34
Monday	23	Gottfried Arnold	2 Pet. 1: 12-2: 3:	10 31	♍ 0	☌ ☽ ♀. ♀ sets 10 10	2	4 35	7 25	4 22
Tuesday	24	John Baptist	James 2:	11 0	♍ 15	♅ rises 12 4	2	4 35	7 25	5 13
Wednesday	25	Augsburg Conf.	" 3:	11 28	♍ 29	Regulus sets 10 30	2	4 35	7 25	5 49
Thursday	26	J. Val. Andreæ	" 4:	11 56	♎ 13	♃ rises 10 53	2	4 35	7 25	6 30
Friday	27	Seven Sleepers	" 5:	morn.	♎ 27	27th. ☿ gr. Hel. Lat. N.	3	4 35	7 25	7 34
Saturday	28	Irenæus	Jude	12 26	♏ 11	♄ rises 12 20	3	4 35	7 25	8 36
26] *3d Sunday after Trinity,*			Luke 15: 1–10; 1 Pet. 5: 5–11.			*Day's Length,* 14 *hours,* 48 *min.*				
Sunday	29	Peter and Paul	Acts 13:	12 59	♏ 25	7* rises 1 42	3	4 36	7 24	9 35
Monday	30	Raymond Lully	" 13: 1–12	1 40	♐ 8	Spica sets 12 8	3	4 36	7 24	10 45

MOON'S PHASES.

Full Moon,	4th, 8 o'clock,	36 min.,	morning.
Last Quarter,	11th, 11	"	58 "	forenoon.
New Moon,	19th, 3	"	22 "	afternoon.
First Quarter,	27th, 12	"	57 "	morning.

CONJECTURES OF THE WEATHER.

1, 2, 3, fair, clear; 4, 5, cloudy; 6, 7, 8, variable; 9, 10, 11, fair; 12, 13, showers; 14, 15, 16, fair; 17, 18, variable; 19, 20, 21, rain; 22, 23, 24, warm; 25, 26, variable; 27, 28, clear; 29, 30, pleasant.

The mechanic feels great interest in his line of work; the sailor loves a ship; the banker eyes piles of money; the artist is at home in colors; and the honest farmer is just a little proud of his choice stock.

OUR FOREIGN MISSION WORK.

The new Board of Foreign Missions, elected by the General Synod, at Lancaster in May 1878, is as follows:

Ministers: Dr. T. S. Johnston, Dr. B. Bausman, Dr. J. H. A. Bomberger, Dr. J. W. Santee, Dr. C. H. Leinbach, Dr. C. Z. Weiser, Dr. D. Van Horne, and Dr. N. Gehr.

Elders: G. S. Griffith, R. F. Kelker, Geo. Gelbach, and W. H. Seibert.

The Board has been organized by the election of the following officers:—*President*, D. Van Horne, D.D.; *Vice-President*, C. H. Leinbach, D.D.; *Corresponding Sec'y*, C. Z. Weiser, D.D.; *Secretary*, T. S. Johnston, D.D.; *Treasurer*, R. F. Kelker.

The Board is anxious to carry out the instructions of the Synod, and send a man or several men to Japan.

May the Lord, prosper this good work! may God move our young men to give themselves to this noble and sacred service!

THE CHURCH.

The Church is our spiritual mother, the body of Christ, the home of the Spirit,—and therefore to be very highly loved, honored, praised and supported.

"Beyond my highest joy
I prize her heavenly ways,
Her sweet Communion, solemn vows,
Her hymns of love and praise."

If we truly love the Church, then we will be interested in her prosperity, in all her work, and will earnestly talk about it, anxiously read about it, faithfully work for it, and devoutly pray for it.

Those who truly love the Church, try regularly to attend public worship, to honor the Church by a godly life, and to uphold her good name among men.

Loving the Church is loving Christ, for the Church is His body (Eph. i. 23).

Some love only their congregation, and others, almost as narrow, care only for their denomination; but this is poor Church-love. Of course every Christian should love his congregation and denomination, but not with bigotry and selfishness; and yet at the same time he must with his whole heart love the whole body of Christ, in heaven and on earth. This is Church-love.

THE CHURCH YEAR.

How beautifully the Church Year presents the facts of redemption, and the effects of redemption; the work of Christ, and the work of the Holy Ghost; the birth of the Church, and its growth; the birth of the Christian, and the development of his Christian life!

Thus the first half is about Christ, and tells what He did in the flesh; the second half is about His Church, and tells what He does by the Spirit.

☞ Never let your pastor feel that he is neglected. Often when he is very tired, and tried, and anxious, a word of sympathy or some other little attention is like sweet sunshine to his soul. He is the Lord's anointed; and in after years it will be very pleasant to know that you were kind to him.

15

JULY, *7th Month, 31 Days.* 1879.

Weeks and Days.		Remarkable Days.	Daily Bible Lessons.	Moon R & S h. m.	Moon's Place. s. a.	Moon's Phases, Aspects of Planets, &c.	s. sl. m.	Sun rises. h. m.	Sun Sets. h. m.	High Water Phila. h. m.
Tuesday	1	H. Voes	Acts 14: 13–52	2 31	21	☽ in per. ♃ sta. ⌒	3	4 36	7 24	11 40
Wednesday	2	Visit V. M.	" 15:	3 16	4	⊙ in Apogee ⌣	4	4 37	7 23	12 20
Thursday	3	Otto Bishop	" 16:	☽ rise	17	3d. ♀ sets 9 50	4	4 37	7 23	1 15
Friday	4	*Independence*	" 17:	8 18	0	♅ rises 11 39	4	4 37	7 23	1 53
Saturday	5	Lord Cobham	" 17:15-18:11	8 48	12	☊. ♄ rises 11 59	4	4 38	7 22	2 31

27] *4th Sunday after Trinity,* Luke 6: 36–42; Rom. 8: 18–23. *Day's Length,* 14 *hours,* 44 *min.*

Sunday	6	John Huss	1 Thess. 1:	9 13	24	Wega south 11 26	4	4 38	7 22	3 30
Monday	7	Willabald	" 2: 1-16:	9 39	6	□ ♄ ⊙	4	4 39	7 21	4 15
Tuesday	8	Kilian	" 2: 17-3:	10 0	18	☌ ☽ ♃. ♃ rises 10 14	5	4 39	7 21	4 50
Wednesday	9	Ephraim the Syr.	" 4:	10 23	29	♅ in Perihelion	5	4 40	7 20	5 44
Thursday	10	Wm. of Orange	" 5:	10 44	11	♄ rises 11 31 [rises 11 0]	5	4 40	7 20	6 30
Friday	11	Placedus	2 " 1: 2: 1-12	11 6	23	11. ☽ ☌ ♄. ♅. ♅	5	4 41	7 19	7 21
Saturday	12	Henry II.	" 2: 13–3	11 26	6	☽ in apo. ♀ sets 9 42	5	4 41	7 19	8 10

28] *5th Sunday after Trinity,* Luke 5: 1–11; 1 Pet. 3: 8–15. *Day's Length,* 14 *hours,* 30 *min.*

Sunday	13	Eugenius	Gala. 1: 1–10	11 59	19	Altair south 12 13	5	4 42	7 18	8 49
Monday	14	Bonaventura	Acts 18: 12; 19: 1-10	morn.	1	Antares south 8 14	6	4 43	7 17	9 36
Tuesday	15	Answer	Gala. 1: 11; 2: 1-14	12 28	14	7* rises 12 34	6	4 43	7 17	10 20
Wednesday	16	Anna Askow	" 2: 15; 3: 1-14	1 15	28	♀ gr. Elon. East ⌒	6	4 44	7 16	10 59
Thursday	17	Separatus & 11 co.	" 3: 15	2 12	19	♄ rises 10 58	6	4 45	7 15	11 42
Friday	18	Arnulf	" 4:	3 18	26	♃ rises 9 44	6	4 46	7 14	12 27
Saturday	19	Louisa Henrietta	" 5: 6:	☽ sets	11	19th. ☊. ♀ in ☊	6	4 46	7 14	1 29

29] *6th Sunday after Trinity,* Matt. 5: 20–26; Rom. 6: 3–11. *Day's Length,* 14 *hours,* 26 *min.*

Sunday	20	John Martheil	1 Cor. 1:	8 21	26	Dog Days Begin	6	4 47	7 13	2 8
Monday	21	Eberhard	" 2:	8 47	11	☌ ☽ ☿. ♅ rises 10 50	6	4 48	7 12	2 46
Tuesday	22	Mary Magdalen	" 3:	9 15	25	□ ♅ ⊙. ☌ ☽ ♀. ♀ [illegible]	6	4 49	7 11	3 30
Wednesday	23	Godfr. v Hamelle	" 4: 5-5: 1-8	9 40	9	⊙ enters ♌	6	4 49	7 11	4 15
Thursday	24	Thos. A. Kempis	" 5: 9–6	10 9	24	Autares south 8 7	6	4 50	7 10	4 55
Friday	25	St. James	" 7:	10 38	8	♃ rises 9 13	6	4 51	7 9	5 42
Saturday	26	Christopher	" 8: 9:	11 26	21	26th. ♄ rises 10 14	6	4 52	7 8	6 33

30] *7th Sunday after Trinity,* Mark 8: 1–9; Rom. 6: 19–23. *Day's Length,* 14 *hours,* 16 *min.*

Sunday	27	Raym Palmarius	1 Cor. 10: 11–1	morn.	5	☽ in per. ☿ gr. Elon. E.	6	4 52	7 8	7 21
Monday	28	Jno. Seb. Bach	" 11: 2	12 16	18	☿ sets 8 0	6	4 53	7 7	8 24
Tuesday	29	Olaus	" 12: 1–30	1 10	1	♄ stationary ⌣	6	4 54	7 6	9 26
Wednesday	30	John Wessel	" 12: 31–13	2 8	14	☿ in Aphelion	6	4 55	7 5	10 34
Thursday	31	Jno. Cas. Schade	" 14:	3 4	26	♀ sets 9 0	6	4 55	7 4	11 32

MOON'S PHASES.

Full Moon,	3d,	4 o'clock,	38 min.,	afternoon.
Last Quarter,	11th,	3 "	55 "	morning.
New Moon,	19th,	4 "	5 "	"
First Quarter,	26th,	5 "	37 "	"

CONJECTURES OF THE WEATHER.

1, 2, fair; 3, 4, 5, showers; 6, 7, 8, warmest days; 9, 10, showers; 11, 12, 13, variable; 14, 15, 16, fair; 17, 18, thunder showers; 19, 20, cloudy; 21, 22, 23, rain; 24, 25, 26, fair; 27, 28, variable; 29, 30, sultry; 31, showers.

Badly scared he is, and with good reason. Dinner on the shady porch is nice; but these buzzing bees and hungry wasps keep one on the watch.

"HE HUMBLED HIMSELF." /

Truly He did so. He laid aside His divinity form, took on Him the form of a servant, and bore our nature ruined by the fall. He was born in a stable, fled to Egypt for His life, ate His bread in the sweat of His face. He was baptized by a sinner, tempted by the devil, hated by the Jews, forsaken by His friends, betrayed, arrested, falsely accused, shamefully insulted, and died even the death of the Cross. Truly "He humbled Himself."

> "Oh sacred Head now wounded,
>   With grief and shame weighed down,
> Now scornfully surrounded,
>   With thorns Thine only Crown."

> "Oh sacred Head what glory,
>   What bliss till now was Thine!
> Yet though despised and gory,
>   I joy to call Thee mine."

OUR PEACE MEASURE.

One of the most important acts of the General Synod of 1878 was the following:

"That a Commission be created by the several District Synods, consisting of a representation .... after the ratio of membership .... partly ministerial and partly lay; which commission, in which the two tendencies shall be proportionately represented, shall consider and solemnly deliberate over all matters in controversy within the Church, with a view of devising a plan of amicable adjustment to be reported to the next General Synod."

The basis of representation was fixed as follows: Synods having 10,000 communicant members or less, one minister and one elder; from 10,000 to 40,000, two ministers and two elders; over 40,000, three ministers and three elders.

In the election of these Commissioners, due regard is to be paid to a minority tendency, if such exist.

Rev. David Van Horne, D. D., President of the General Synod, shall be temporary Chairman of the Commission, which is to convene in Harrisburg, Pa., November 28th, 1879, at 7 P. M.

A majority of the Commission, representing at least four Synods, shall be a quorum.

This is our peace measure. All good hearts are weary of war, and hope for much from this Commission.

In the meantime let us all earnestly pray that the right men may be elected Commissioners, and that they may be enlightened and guided by the Holy Ghost in their work.

ADVICE TO CHOIRS.

Be a Christian. Go regularly to practice. Behave well during service. Never write notes. Never read anything. Don't talk. When done singing, lay your books away. Join in the prayer. Devoutly hear the lesson. Listen to the sermon, like other good people. Feel that you are part of the congregation. Never join in a choir-riot. If any there can sing better than you can, thank God for it. If he thinks he can, but you think otherwise, don't think too loud.

☞ The churches in the United States cost, as nearly as may be estimated, twenty millions a year, or an average of about half a dollar a year to each inhabitant.

17

AUGUST, *8th Month, 31 Days.* 1879.

Weeks and Days.		Remarkable Days.	Daily Bible Lessons.	Moon R & S h. m.	Moon's Place. s.	a.	Moon's Phases, Aspects of Planets, &c.	s. sl. m.	Sun rises. h. m.	Sun sets. h. m.	High Water. Phila. h. m.
Friday	1	Maccabees	1 Cor. 15: 1–34	3 59	♑	9	○ ♀ sets 8 56 ⌣	6	4 57	7 3	12 21
Saturday	2	Mart. under Nero	" 15: 35–16	☽ rise	♑	21	2d. ♅ rises 10 32	6	4 58	7 2	1 17
31] *8th Sunday after Trinity,*		Matt. 7: 15–21; Rom. 8: 12–17.					*Day's Length,* 14 *hours,* 2 *min.*				
Sunday	3	Wm. Thorp	Acts 19: 11-20: 1	7 56	♒	3	☊. Sirius rises 4 34	6	4 59	7 1	2 10
Monday	4	Leonard Käser	2 Cor. 1: 1–22	8 18	♒	15	☌ ☽ ♃. □ Neptune ⊙	6	5 0	7 0	3 4
Tuesday	5	Salzb'g Evang.	" 1: 23–2	8 44	♒	27	♃ rises 8 20	6	5 1	6 59	3 41
Wednesday	6	Transfiguration	" 3: 4: 1–6	9 16	♓	8	7* rises 11 6	6	5 2	6 58	4 30
Thursday	7	Nonna	" 4: 7-5: 10	9 48	♓	20	☌ ☽ ♄. ♄ rises 9 28	5	5 3	6 57	5 24
Friday	8	Hormisdas	" 5: 11; 6: 7: 1	10 15	♈	2	☾ ♅ rises 10 12	5	5 4	6 56	6 12
Saturday	9	Numidicus	" 7: 2	10 44	♈	14	9th. ☽ in apo. ☌ ☽ ♅	5	5 6	6 54	6 44
32] *9th Sunday after Trinity,*		Luke 16: 1–9; 1 Cor. 10: 1–13.					*Day's Length,* 13 *hours,* 46 *min.*				
Sunday	10	Laurentius	2 Cor. 8:	11 10	♈	26	♀ sets 8 47	5	5 7	6 53	7 31
Monday	11	Greg. of Utrecht	" 9:	11 52	♉	10	Rigel rises 2 12	5	5 8	6 52	8 20
Tuesday	12	An. of Havelberg	" 10:	morn.	♉	23	♄ rises 9 0	5	5 9	6 51	8 59
Wednesday	13	C'nt. Zinzendorf	" 11:	12 53	♊	6	♃ rises 7 48 ⌢	5	5 10	6 50	9 43
Thursday	14	James Guthrie	" 12: 1–18	1 59	♊	20	Orion rises 1 48	4	5 11	6 49	10 34
Friday	15	Virgin Mary	" 12: 19-33:	2 46	♋	5	Wega south 8 56	4	5 12	6 48	11 25
Saturday	16	John of Saxony	Acts 20: 1–13	3 36	♋	19	Neptune stationary.	4	5 14	6 46	12 20
33] *10th Sunday after Trinity,*		Luke 19: 41–47; 1 Cor. 12: 1–11.					*Day's Length,* 13 *hours,* 30 *min.*				
Sunday	17	John Gerhard	Rom. 1: 1–17	☽ sets	♌	4	● 17th. ☋. ♄ rises 8 39	4	5 15	6 45	1 15
Monday	18	Hugo Grotius	" 1: 18–31	7 18	♌	19	☌ ☽ ☿. ♅ ris's 9 58	4	5 16	6 44	2 9
Tuesday	19	Sebaldus	" 2:	7 42	♍	4	♀ gr. brilliancy.	3	5 17	6 43	2 55
Wednesday	20	Bernard of Clair.	" 3:	8 9	♍	19	☿ gr. Hel. Lat. S. ☌ ☽ ♀	3	5 18	6 42	3 42
Thursday	21	1st Morv. Mission	" 4:	8 36	♎	4	♀ sets 8 6	3	5 19	6 41	4 31
Friday	22	Symphorianus	" 5: 1–11	9 28	♎	8	☽ in per. ♀ in Aphelion	3	5 21	6 39	5 16
Saturday	23	Gasp. de Coligne	" 5: 12–21	10 12	♏	2	☌ ☿ ⊙ Infr. ⊙ ent'rs ♍	2	5 22	6 38	5 56
34] *11th Sunday after Trinity,*		Luke 18: 9–14; 1 Cor. 15: 1–11.					*Day's Length,* 13 *hours,* 14 *min.*				
Sunday	24	Bartholomew	Rom. 6:	11 4	♏	16	☽ 24th. ♃ rises 7 10	2	5 23	6 37	6 42
Monday	25	Louis IX.	" 7:	11 52	♏	29	Sirius rises 3 22 ⌣	2	5 24	6 36	7 35
Tuesday	26	Ulfilas	" 8: 1–15	morn.	♐	11	♄ rises 8 1	1	5 25	6 35	8 31
Wednesday	27	Jovinian	" 8: 16–39	12 50	♐	23	♅ rises 9 40	1	5 26	6 34	9 29
Thursday	28	Aug. of Hippo	" 9: 1–13	1 54	♑	5	☌ ✱ ⊙	1	5 27	6 33	10 26
Friday	29	St. John Bapt.	" 9: 14–33	2 56	♑	17	☊. ♀ sets 7 48	0	5 28	6 32	11 24
Saturday	30	Claud of Turin	" 10:	3 59	♑	29	Dog Days end.	0	5 30	6 30	12 21
35] *12th Sunday after Trinity,*		Mark 7: 31–37; 2 Cor. 3: 4–11.					*Day's Length,* 12 *hours,* 58 *min.*				
Sunday	31	Aidan	Rom. 11:	☽ rise	♒	11	○ 31st. ☍ ♃ ⊙. ☌ ☽ ♃	0	5 31	6 29	1 18

MOON'S PHASES.

Full Moon,	2d,	2 o'clock,	13 min.	morning.
Last Quarter,	9th,	9 "	10 "	evening.
New Moon,	17th,	3 "	11 "	afternoon.
First Quarter,	24th,	10 "	12 "	forenoon.
Full Moon,	31st,	1 "	56 "	afternoon.

CONJECTURES OF THE WEATHER.

1, 2, showers; 3, 4, 5, fair; 6, 7, 8, showers; 9, 10, variable; 11, 12, 13, clear; 14, cloudy; 15, 16, rain; 17, 18, 19, fair; 20, 21, 22, variable; 23, 24, 25, fair; 26, rain; 28, 28, fair; 29, 30, cloudy, rainy; 31, fair and clear.

(♃). Jupiter is in opposition with the Sun the 31st of this month, nearest to the earth, and shines all night.

A DINNER AND A KISS.

"I have brought your dinner, father,"
The blacksmith's daughter said,
As she took from her arm the kettle,
And lifted its shining lid.
"There is not any pie or pudding,
So I will give you this;"
And upon his toil-worn forehead
She left a loving kiss.

The blacksmith took off his apron,
And dined in happy mood,
Wondering much at the savor,
Hid in his humble food;
While all about him were visions
Full of prophetic bliss;
But he never thought of the magic
In his little daughter's kiss.

While she with her kettle swinging,
Merrily trudged away,
Stopping at sight of a squirrel,
Catching some wild bird's lay,—
O, I thought, how many a shadow
Of life and of fate we would miss,
If always our frugal dinners
Were seasoned with a kiss!

THE AGE OF OUR MINISTERS.

The following facts are taken from the Western Reformed Church Almanac of 1878:

Nearly half of our Ministers have been ordained within ten years.

About six have been in the Ministry forty years; ten or twelve have been Pastors for fifty years; and one, Rev. George Leidy, of Norristown, Pa., was ordained sixty years ago.

The average age of our deceased Ministers is remarkable, as the following table will show:—

1870	Died,	6	Average Age,	63.
1871	"	11	"	" 61.
1872	"	7	"	" 56.
1873	"	5	"	" 58.
1874	"	9	"	" 64.
1875	"	14	"	" 66.
1876	"	13	"	" 52.
1877	"	10	"	" 63.
1878	"	9	"	" 64.

Died, 84.   Average Age, 61.

This, indeed, is the average age of American Ministers in general.

SPECIAL THANK-OFFERINGS.

Nothing is more beautiful and proper in the Christian life, than to give the Lord special thank-offerings for special mercies.

If a man saves your life, or the life of your child, or does any other great act for you, how gladly you give him a large reward!

How much more, then, we need to acknowledge God's goodness in thankful gifts—for the recovery of self or child from sickness, or deliverance from any great trial (as did David, Ps. 66 : 13-15).

"I beseech you therefore brethren *by the mercies of God.*" (Rom. 12 : 1.)

Such special thank-offerings are very proper in our "harvest-home" services, as a devout and grateful acknowledgment that all the fruits of the earth are from the hand of God. (Ps. 65 : 9-13.)

How largely, as well as sincerely, we should then give alms, even as the Lord hath prospered us!

☞ Many Christians from sweet experience know that it is a good thing to break the six common days into two parts, and put a sacred service between them on Wednesday Evening.

19

SEPTEMBER, *9th Month, 30 Days.* 1879.

Weeks and Days.		Remarkable Days.	Daily Bible Lessons.	Moon R & S h. m.	Moon's Place. s. a.	Moon's Phases, Aspects of Planets, &c.	s. fs. m.	Sun rises. h. m.	Sun sets. h. m.	HIGH WATER. Phila. h. m.
Monday	1	Hanna	Rom. 12:	6 47	♓ 23	☊. ☿ stationary	0	5 32	6 28	2 9
Tuesday	2	Mamas	" 13:	7 10	♈ 5	♀ sets 7 28	0	5 33	6 27	2 46
Wednesday	3	Hildegarde	" 14:	7 38	♈ 17	☌ ☽ ♄. ♄ rises 7 39	1	5 35	6 25	3 34
Thursday	4	Ida	" 15: 1–13	8 4	♈ 29	Neptune gr. Hel. Lat. S.	1	5 36	6 24	4 18
Friday	5	John Mollio	" 15: 14–33	8 36	♉ 11	♅ rises 9 14	1	5 37	6 23	4 58
Saturday	6	Martin Weibel	" 16:	9 12	♉ 23	☽ in apo. ☌ ☽ ♅	2	5 39	6 21	5 40
36] 13*th Sunday after Trinity,*			Luke 10: 23–27; Gal. 3: 16–22.			*Day's Length,* 12 *hours,* 40 *min.*				
Sunday	7	Laz. Spengler	Acts 20:	9 59	♊ 5	♃ south 11 30	2	5 40	6 20	6 21
Monday	8	Corbinian	" 21:	10 54	♊ 18	8th. ☿ in ☊	2	5 41	6 19	6 59
Tuesday	9	Lorigi Paschall	" 22: 23:	11 53	♋ 1	☿ gr. elon. W.	3	5 43	6 17	7 44
Wednesday	10	Paul Separatus	" 24: 25:	morn.	♋ 14	☿ rises 4 49	3	5 44	6 16	8 32
Thursday	11	John Brenz	" 26:	1 4	♋ 29	Wega south 7 16	3	5 45	6 15	9 98
Friday	12	Diony's Peloq'n	" 27:	2 18	♌ 13	☿ in Perihelion	4	5 46	6 14	10 9
Saturday	13	Wm. Farel	" 28:	3 10	♌ 28	♄ rises 7 8	4	5 48	6 12	10 49
37] 14*th Sunday after Trinity,*			Luke 17: 11–19; Gal. 5: 16–24.			*Day's Length,* 12 *hours,* 22 *min.*				
Sunday	14	Cyprian	Eph. 1: 1–14	4 4	♍ 13	☋. ☌ ☽ ☿. ☿ Hel. Lat. S.	4	5 49	6 11	11 38
Monday	15	Av. v. Grumb'h	" 1: 15; 2: 1-10	4 54	♍ 28	Antares sets 9 12	5	5 50	6 10	12 34
Tuesday	16	Euphemia	" 2: 11–3	☽ sets	♎ 13	16th. ☌ ☽ ☿. ♅ rises 8 50	5	5 52	6 8	1 31
Wednesday	17	*Ember Day*	" 4: 1–17	6 48	♎ 28	♃ south 10 52	6	5 53	6 7	2 20
Thursday	18	A. G. Spangeb'g	" 4: 18	7 15	♏ 13	☽ in per.	6	5 54	6 6	3 14
Friday	19	Thos. of St. Paul	" 5: 6: 1-9	8 12	♏ 27	7* rises 8 26	6	5 56	6 4	4 4
Saturday	20	Magdal. Luther	" 6: 10	9 4	♐ 11	Antares sets 8 48	7	5 57	6 3	4 48
38] 15*th Sunday after Trinity,*			Matt. 6: 24–34; Gal. 5: 25; 6: 10.			*Day's Length,* 12 *hours,* 4 *min.*				
Sunday	21	Matthew	Colos. 1:	9 54	♐ 24	Sirius rises 1 41	7	5 58	6 2	5 36
Monday	22	Mauritius	" 2: 3: 1-4	10 51	♑ 7	22d. Spica sets 6 45	7	5 59	6 1	6 29
Tuesday	23	Mart. of Genoa	" 3: 5–4	11 50	♑ 20	☉ ent. ♎. D. & N. equal ☌ ☿ ☉	8	6 0	6 0	7 19
Wednesday	24	Jno. Jacob Moser	Philemon	morn.	♒ 2	Autumn com. ☾ infer.	8	6 2	5 58	8 10
Thursday	25	Augsb'g Treaty	Philip 1: 1–26	12 51	♒ 14	☊. ♀ rises 8 29	8	6 3	5 57	9 4
Friday	26	Lioba	" 1: 27–2:	1 52	♒ 26	Fomal south 10 38	9	6 4	5 56	9 46
Saturday	27	Phil. Graveron	" 3: 4:	2 56	♓ 8	☌ ☽ ♃. ♃ south 10 10	9	6 6	5 54	10 36
39] 16*th Sunday after Trinity,*			Luke 7: 11–17; Eph. 4: 1–6.			*Day's Length,* 11 *hours,* 46 *min.*				
Sunday	28	A. Clarenbach	1 Tim. 1:	3 59	♓ 20	Aldebaran rises 9 12	9	6 7	5 53	11 32
Monday	29	St. Michael	" 2:	5 4	♈ 2	7* rises 7 50	10	6 8	5 52	12 29
Tuesday	30	Jerome	" 3:	☽ rise	♈ 14	30th. ☌ ☽ ♃	10	6 10	5 50	1 26

MOON'S PHASES.

Last Quarter, 8th, 3 o'clock, 5 min., afternoon.
New Moon, 16th, 12 " 57 " morning.
First Quarter, 22d, 4 " 22 " evening.
Full Moon, 30th, 4 " 19 " morning.

CONJECTURES OF THE WEATHER.

1, 2, fair; 3, showers; 4, 5, fair; 6, 7, variable; 8, 9, fair; 10, showers; 11, 12, varinble; 13, 14, rain; 15, 16, variable; 17, 18, fair; 19, cloudy; 20, 21, 22, clear; 23, 24, 25, variable; 26, 27, 28, fair; 29, 30, showers.

(♀) Venus is Inferior conjunction with the Sun. Passes from Evening Star to Morning Star.

What an odd bird! It is found in New Zealand, and the natives call it kirvi-kirvi. Its wings are so small that they are hard to find; and it has no tail at all. Its nose is at the tip of its bill. It lives mainly among ferns, digging worms with its toes.

"THEY ALL .... BEGAN TO MAKE EXCUSE."

So to-day yet. Men do not object to the Gospel, but only neglect it. They make no open opposition, but only show deep indifference to it. Many would feel much hurt if you should call them the enemies of Christianity; and yet they never come to the great feast. They all make excuse.

One man thinks it is not necessary. Another feels unfit. Another is waiting till he is sure he can keep his vows. One stumbles at unworthy members, and another is halting between denominations, while many think there is yet plenty of time.

All these excuses are foolish, empty and very dangerous. They help to harden the heart. They imply that if these things were out of the way men would come to Christ in His Church; but not so. They are in fact not real difficulties, but only off-comes, to satisfy conscience and shut the mouth of God's minister.

The real and true reason for not being in the Church is an unbelieving heart, a disobedient spirit, an unwillingness to forsake sin and follow after holiness.

A FEW QUESTIONS FOR CONSISTORIES.

Do we pay our pastor salary enough? Do we pay him regularly, according to our promise in the call? Have we any right to expect him to help to collect it? Have we any right to make him take half of it in trade? And if he takes trade, have members a right to charge him the very highest market price? Do we know what the Constitution says about this matter? Do we really care for his comfort? How shall we account to the Lord for our treatment of His anointed?

☞ Nearly half of our Ministers live in Pennsylvania. About one-fourth live in Ohio. The rest are scattered over twenty-five States and Territories.

AS TRUE NOW AS THEN.

"*Nor can the German Reformed Church excuse herself from taking her part in it. She owes it to herself—to her best interests. May every one of her members feel it to be, not only a duty, but a privilege to take an active and lively interest in it.*"

These words, in regard to Foreign Missions, are as true now as they were thirty-two years ago. They close the essay of Rev. Dr. Benj. Schneider, published in LETTERS FROM BROOSA, in 1846. At that time our Church had some zeal in Foreign Missions. The Lord revive in us this holy zeal.

☞ Beware of your first thought or temptation to neglect the Lord's Supper. The first yielding makes the second more easy.

OCTOBER, *10th Month, 31 Days.* 1879.

Weeks and Days.		Remarkable Days.	Daily Bible Lessons.	Moon R & S h. m.	Moon's Place s. ●	°	Moon's Phases, Aspects of Planets, &c.	S. fs. m.	Sun rises. h. m.	Sun Sets. h. m.	High Water. Phila. h. m.
Wednesday	1	Remigius	1 Tim. 3: 14-4: 10	6 29	♈	26	♃ south 9 50 ◡	10	6 11	5 49	2 16
Thursday	2	Chr. Schmid	" 4: 11-5: 16	6 59	♉	8	Sirius rises 1 6	11	6 12	5 48	2 54
Friday	3	The two Ewaldes	" 5: 17	7 31	♉	20	♅ rises 8 4	11	6 13	5 47	3 44
Saturday	4	Franciscus	" 6:	8 14	♊	2	☽ in apo. ☌ ☽ ♅	11	6 15	5 45	4 33
40] *17th Sunday after Trinity,*		Luke 14: 1–11; Eph. 4: 1–6.	*Day's Length,* 11 *hours,* 28 *min.*								
Sunday	5	Petro Carnesec	Titus 1:	8 59	♊	15	☍ ♄ ☉. ☌ ☿ ☉ superi'r	12	6 16	5 44	5 20
Monday	6	Henry Albert	" 2:	9 40	♊	28	♅ stationary ◠	12	6 17	5 43	6 10
Tuesday	7	Theodore Beza	" 3:	10 34	♋	11	♄ south 12 0	12	6 18	5 42	6 49
Wednesday	8	Robt. of Lincoln	2 Tim. 1:	11 12	♋	24	☾ 8th. ♃ south 9 18	12	6 19	5 41	7 35
Thursday	9	Dionysius Areo.	" 2:	morn.	♌	7	Altair south 6 43	13	6 20	5 40	8 24
Friday	10	Justus Jonas	" 3:	12 12	♌	21	☋. Orion rises 10 20	13	6 21	5 39	9 12
Saturday	11	Ulrich Zwingli	" 4:	1 24	♍	6	♅ rises 7 44	13	6 23	5 37	9 49
41] *18th Sunday after Trinity,*		Matt. 22: 34–46: 1 Cor. 1: 4–9.	*Day's Length,* 11 *hours,* 12 *min.*								
Sunday	12	Henry Bullinger	Heb. 1:	2 46	♍	21	♀ stationary	13	6 24	5 36	10 40
Monday	13	Elizabeth Fry	" 2:	3 59	♎	6	☌ ☽ ♀. ♀ rises 4 36	14	6 26	5 34	11 35
Tuesday	14	Nich. Ridley	" 3: 4:	5 10	♎	21	7* rises 6 54	14	6 27	5 33	12 28
Wednesday	15	Aurelia	" 5:	☽ sets	♏	6	● 15th. ♃ so. 8 46	14	6 29	5 31	1 21
Thursday	16	Gallus	" 6:	5 56	♏	21	☽ in per. ☌ ☽ ☿	14	6 31	5 29	2 11
Friday	17	Rv. Edict of Nan.	" 7:	6 39	♐	6	Capella south 3 40	15	6 32	5 28	2 47
Saturday	18	St. Luke, Ev.	" 8:	7 31	♐	20	♄ south 12 22	15	6 33	5 27	3 34
42] *19th Sunday after Trinity,*		Matt. 9: 1–8; Eph. 4: 17–32.	*Day's Length,* 10 *hours,* 52 *min.*								
Sunday	19	Bruno	Heb. 9: 1–14	8 36	♑	4	♅ rises 7 20 ◡	15	6 34	5 26	4 22
Monday	20	F. Lamb't of Avi.	" 9: 15	9 44	♑	17	♀ rises 4 10	15	6 36	5 24	5 11
Tuesday	21	Hilarion	" 10: 1–18	10 59	♑	29	Sirius rises 11 54	15	6 37	5 23	5 56
Wednesday	22	Hedwig	" 10: 19–39	morn.	♒	11	☽ 22d. ☊. ☉ ent. ♏	15	6 38	5 22	6 42
Thursday	23	Henry Martin.	" 11:	12 59	♒	23	Andromeda south 10 10	16	6 40	5 20	7 31
Friday	24	Arethas	" 12:	1 52	♓	5	☌ ☽ ♃. ♃ south 8 16	16	6 41	5 19	8 29
Saturday	25	John Herz	" 13:	2 54	♓	17	Orion rises 9 25	16	6 42	5 18	9 27
43] *20th Sunday after Trinity,*		Matt. 22: 1–14; Eph. 5: 15–21.	*Day's Length,* 10 *hours,* 34 *min.*								
Sunday	26	Frederick III.	Prov. 1: 2:	3 55	♓	29	☿ in Aphelion	16	6 43	5 17	10 24
Monday	27	Frumentius	" 3:	4 56	♈	11	♄ south 11 12	16	6 44	5 16	11 19
Tuesday	28	Simon and Jude	" 4:	5 57	♈	23	☌ ☽ ♄. ♃ stationary	16	6 45	5 15	12 17
Wednesday	29	Alfred the Great	" 5: 6; 1-19:	☽ rises	♉	5	○ 29th. ♀ rises 3 47	16	6 46	5 14	1 16
Thursday	30	Jacob Sturm	" 6: 20-7	5 40	♉	17	♀ gr. Brilliancy	16	6 48	5 12	2 0
Friday	31	Fest. of Reform'n	" 8:	6 16	♉	29	☽ in apo. ☌ ☽ ♅. ♅ [illegible]	16	6 49	5 11	2 32

MOON'S PHASES.

Last Quarter,	8th,	8 o'clock,	45 min.,	morning.
New Moon,	15th,	10 "	9 "	forenoon.
First Quarter,	22d,	1 "	19 "	morning.
Full Moon,	29th,	9 "	10 "	evening.

CONJECTURES OF THE WEATHER.

1, 2, fair; 3, cloudy; 4, 5, fair; 6, 7, rain; 8, 9, 10, clear; 11, 12, cloudy; 13, 14, rain; 15, 16, 17, fair; 18, 19, variable; 20, 21, 22, clear; 23, variable; 24, 25, 26, fair; 27, 28, rain; 29, 30, 31, fair.

(♄) Saturn is in opposition with the Sun, the 5th of this month, and shines all night.

Good manners are so nice! The bell rings and Harry meets this lady at the door. He shows her into the parlor, bids her be seated, and excuses himself to call mamma. Good manners win where fine clothes fail.

VERY STRANGE.

A congregation pays a pastor a certain salary, and perhaps even this in dribs, irregularly and unkindly; but when a new man is called, lo! at once the salary is raised.

How strange this is! And how wrong it is! The old pastor likely did much for the congregation, giving them his best years. The new man, who has done nothing for them, is at once raised above the level of the old.

Is this right? Is it just between man and man? Congregations should never forget that the Holy Saviour expects and demands that His servants be fairly treated—to say the very least—and part of this is a kind appreciation of their services.

THE REFORMATION FESTIVAL.

This is October 31st. The day is not so much observed and honored in the Reformed as in the Lutheran Church; but it deserves great notice, for on the evening of that day, in 1517, Luther nailed his noted ninety-five theses to the door of the Electoral Church in Wittenberg, Germany—his first public attack on the errors of the Roman Catholic Church.

Read and study the history of the Reformation, and you will plainly see these four facts:

1) *How necessary it was.* The people were very ignorant of the Scriptures, and their priests were notoriously wicked.

2) *God had prepared the way for a great work.* He had Reformers before the Reformation; and printing was invented just in time to be of great service in spreading the truth.

3) *The Reformation was universal.* It arose in Switzerland and Germany in 1516 and 1517, but very soon spread all over Europe. What better evidence of God's hand in it than this?

4) *Its gradual progress.* Step by step Zwingli, Luther, Calvin and others were led on, much further than they at first expected to go, and truly by a way they knew not. It cost much time, even blood and tears, but God has owned it.

TAKE YOUR CERTIFICATE.

One bad custom in some parts of the Church is this, that members moving from one charge to another, do not remove their membership.

Now, the Constitution of our Church, in article 130, says: "Members of the Church removing from the bounds of one congregation to those of another, shall obtain a certificate of membership and dismission, and connect themselves at the earliest opportunity with the congregation to whose bounds they have removed."

Hence, the congregation to which they move has a right to expect them to do so; and it is a plain duty, too, because members have no proper right to church privileges so long as they refuse to stand in right relation to the congregation.

Their own pastor, too, should urge them to take their certificate of dismission. Instead of this lawful, orderly and just way, however, many members care not to be dismissed, and many pastors even try to hold their members.

NOVEMBER, *11th Month, 30 Days.* 1879.

Weeks and Days.		Remarkable Days.	Daily Bible Lessons.	Moon R & S h. m.	Moon's Place. s.	a.	Moon's Phases, Aspects of Planets, &c.	s. fs. m.	Sun rises. h. m.	Sun Sets. h. m.	HIGH WATER. Phila. h. m.
Saturday	1	All Saints	Prov. 9:	6 58	♊	12	♃ south 7 54 ◡	16	6 50	5 10	3 16
44] *4th Sunday before Advent,*			Matt. 9: 18–26; Col. 1: 9–14.				*Day's Length,* 10 *hours,* 18 *min.*				
Sunday	2	Victorinus	John 21: 1–23	7 55	♊	25	♀ rises 3 40 ◠	16	6 51	5 9	5 56
Monday	3	Pirminus	1 John 1: 2:	8 59	♋	8	☍ Neptune ☉	16	6 53	5 7	4 43
Tuesday	4	John a Bengel	" 3:	10 7	♋	21	♂ rises 6 40	16	6 54	5 6	5 31
Wednesday	5	Hans Egede	" 4:	11 16	♌	11	♄ south 10 37	16	6 55	5 5	6 20
Thursday	6	Gustav. Adolph's	" 5:	morn.	♌	17	7* south 12 51 ☋.	16	6 56	5 4	6 54
Friday	7	Willibrord	2 John	12 28	♍	1	7th. Sirius r. 10 48	16	6 57	5 3	7 41
Saturday	8	Willehad	3 John	1 39	♍	16	Aldebaran so. 1 35	16	6 58	5 2	8 38
45] *3d Sunday before Advent,*			Matt. 24: 15–28; 1 Thess. 4: 13–18.				*Day's Length,* 10 *hours,* 2 *min.*				
Sunday	9	John v. Staupitz	Rev. 1:	2 29	♎	1	♀ in ☊. ♂ in ☊.	16	6 59	5 1	9 32
Monday	10	Martin Luther	" 2:	3 10	♎	16	☌ ☽ ♀. ♀ rises 3 29	16	7 0	5 0	10 22
Tuesday	11	Martin of Tours	" 3:	4 19	♏	1	♃ south 7 24	16	7 1	4 59	11 21
Wednesday	12	Phil. de Mornay	" 4: 5; 6:	5 28	♏	15	☍ ♂ ☉. ♂ south 11 49	16	7 2	4 58	12 20
Thursday	13	Arcadius	" 7; 8; 9; 1-12	☽ sets	♏	29	13th. ☽ in per.	16	7 3	4 57	1 15
Friday	14	Pet. Mart. Vern.	" 9: 13-10; 11:	5 10	♐	14	Rigel rises 8 28	15	7 4	4 56	1 57
Saturday	15	John Kepler	" 12: 13:	6 15	♐	28	☌ ☽ ☿. ♄ so. 10 2 ◡	15	7 5	4 55	2 43
46] *2d Sunday before Advent,*			Matt. 25: 31–46; 2 Thess. 3: 1–10.				*Day's Length,* 9 *hours,* 48 *min.*				
Sunday	16	Casp. Creuziger	Rev. 14: 1-13	7 21	♑	12	☿ gr. Hel. Lat. S.	15	7 6	4 54	3 31
Monday	17	Bernward	" 14: 14–20	8 26	♑	25	♃ south 6 59	15	7 7	4 53	4 20
Tuesday	18	Greg. Illuminat.	" 15:	9 32	♒	8	☊. ♀ rises 3 20	15	7 8	4 52	5 10
Wednesday	19	Elizab. of Hesse	" 16: 1–8	10 35	♒	19	♂ south 11 32	14	7 9	4 51	5 55
Thursday	20	John Williams	" 16: 9–21	11 39	♓	1	20th. ☉ enters ♂	14	7 10	4 50	6 44
Friday	21	Columbanus	" 17:	morn.	♓	13	☌ ☽ ♃. ☿ gr. Elon. East	14	7 11	4 49	7 34
Saturday	22	John Oecolampadius	" 18:	12 46	♓	25	☿ sets 5 33	14	7 12	4 48	8 26
47] *1st Sunday before Advent,*			Matth. 25: 1–13; 2 Pet. 3: 3–14.				*Day's Length,* 9 *hours,* 34 *min.*				
Sunday	23	Clemens Roman.	Rev. 19: 1–10	1 59	♈	7	Orion rises 7 23	13	7 13	4 47	9 16
Monday	24	John Knox	" 19: 11-20: 1-3	3 12	♈	19	☌ ☽ ♄. ♄ south 9 30	13	7 14	4 46	10 12
Tuesday	25	Catharine	" 20: 4–15	4 16	♉	1	♀ rises 3 18	13	7 15	4 45	10 49
Wednesday	26	Conrad	" 21: 1–8	5 24	♉	13	□ ♃ ☉. ♃ south 6 29	12	7 16	4 44	11 34
Thursday	27	Marg't Blaurer	" 21: 9–22	6 22	♉	26	☽ in apo. ☌ ☽ ♂	12	7 17	4 43	12 22
Friday	28	Alex. Roussel	Psalm 96	☽ rise	♊	8	28th. ♂ south 11 4	12	7 17	4 43	1 16
Saturday	29	Satarinus	" 145	5 20	♊	21	♃ sets 11 14	11	7 18	4 42	2 6
48] *1st Sunday in Advent,*			Matt. 21: 8–11; Rom. 13: 11–14.				*Day's Length,* 9 *hours,* 24 *min.*				
Sunday	30	St. Andrew	John 1: 1-14	6 28	♋	4	☿ stationary ◠	11	7 18	4 42	2 46

MOON'S PHASES.

Last Quarter.	7th,	12 o'clock,		56 min.,		morning.
New Moon,	13th,	7	"	38	"	evening.
First Quarter,	20th,	1	"	56	"	afternoon.
Full Moon,	28th	3	"	59	"	evening.

CONJECTURES OF THE WEATHER.

1, 2, variable; 3, rainy; 4, 5, 6, clear; 7, 8, moderate; 9, 10, cloudy; 11, rain; 12, 13, 14, fair; 15, 16, variable; 17, cloudy; 18, 19, rain; 20, 21, 22, fair; 23, showers; 24, 25, variable; 26, 27, 28, cold, rain, snow; 29, 30, clear, c'ld.

(♂). Mars is in apposition with the Sun, the 12th of this month, and shines all night.

How nice, when boys and girls are fond of books! They have so much pleasure on long evenings and rainy days. But some people do not take good care of books. They toss them about like so much trash, and spoil them more that they use them.

AN OLD THANKSGIVING PROCLAMATION.

The Congress of the United States in October, 1779, adopted the following resolution:

"*Resolved*, That it be recommended to the several States, to appoint Thursday, the 9th of December next, to be a day of public and solemn thanksgiving to Almighty God for his mercies, and of prayer for the continuance of his favor and protection to these United States; to beseech him that he would be graciously pleased to influence our public councils, and bless them with wisdom from on high, with unanimity, firmness and success; that he would go forth with our hosts, and crown our armies with victory; that he would grant to his church the plentiful effusion of divine grace, and pour out his Holy Spirit on all ministers of the gospel; that he would bless and prosper the means of education, and spread the light of Christian knowledge through the remotest corners of the earth; that he would smile upon the labors of his people, and cause the earth to bring forth her fruits in abundance, that we may with gratitude and gladness enjoy them; . . . that he would in mercy look down upon us, pardon our sins, and receive us into his favor; and finally, that he would establish the independence of these United States upon the basis of religion and virtue, and support and protect them in the enjoyment of peace, liberty and safety."

Study these words carefully. They sound very much as if that old Congress had been a Christian body. Why cannot our rulers now frame such sentences? Have they a different spirit, or are they afraid?

"WATCH, THEREFORE."

"Behold the Bridegroom cometh in the middle of the night,
And blest is he whose loins are girt, whose lamp is burning bright;
But woe to that dull servant whom the Master shall surprise,
With lamp untrimmed, unburning, and with slumber in his eyes.

Beware, my soul; beware, beware, lest thou in slumber lie,
And, like the five, remain without, and knock, and wait, and cry;
But watch, and bear thy lamp undimmed, and Christ shall gird thee on,
His own bright wedding-robe of light—tho glory of the Son."

Foolish virgins are all around us. Many people profess to be friends of the Bridegroom, but care not for His coming, and will some day be startled by the cry, "Behold, He cometh."

Many young people in the Church are living very carelessly. Many older are full of business and care, cumbered with much serving, and seem not to know that the night cometh.

"Waiting for the coming of our Lord Jesus Christ," is a very joyful and sacred privilege of Christians. During the year some dear saints have gone to heaven. They wait there, while we watch and wait here. But soon the waiting will end, and the cry will be made, "Behold the Bridegroom cometh." Then all faithful souls shall rise to meet Him, and with joy shall enter in with Him to the marriage-feast.

But what of those who are not His friends?—who have never waited for Him?—who have not so much as honored Him here? They will be shut out.

FOR THE BOYS AND GIRLS.

Now the evenings are getting long, and you must stay in the house. Have the good habit of using your evenings in reading and study. You may do much in a single winter. Have a book always at hand. Have the place marked with a slip of paper, and begin right there. Even if you can read only half an hour do that. Years are made up of half hours, and life of little things. Read your Bible daily, in short parts. Read the Church paper. Have your hymn-book near, and read or sing a hymn. Do this, and see how pleasantly the winter will pass away, and how much you will learn in six months.

25

DECEMBER, *12th Month, 31 Days.* 1879.

Weeks and Days.		Remarkable Days.	Daily Bible Lessons.	Moon R & S h. m.	Moon's Place s.	a.	Moon's Phases, Aspects of Planets, &c.	s. fa. m.	Sun rises. h. m.	Sun sets. h. m.	HIGH WATER Phila. h. m.
Monday	1	Eligius	Gen. 2: 4-25	7 40	♋	18	□ ♅ ☉. ♀ rises 8 24 ⌒	11	7 19	4 41	3 34
Tuesday	2	John Ruysbruck	Matt. 19: 1-12	8 51	♌	3	☋. ♅ south 10 56	10	7 19	4 41	4 26
Wednesday	3	Gerhard Groot	Eph. 5: 22-33	9 59	♌	17	♃ sets 11 1	10	7 20	4 40	5 14
Thursday	4	Gerh. v. Zutphen	1 Cor. 7:	11 16	♍	1	♀ gr. Elon. West	10	7 20	4 40	5 46
Friday	5	Crispin	Gen. 3:	morn.	♍	16	7* south 10 52	9	7 21	4 39	6 30
Saturday	6	Nicholas	" 8: 15-9: 17	12 29	♍	29	6th. Sirius r. 8 48	9	7 21	4 39	7 16

49] *2d Sunday in Advent,* Luke 21 : 25–33 ; Rom. 15 : 4–13. *Day's Length,* 9 *hours,* 16 *min.*

Sunday	7	Paulus Odontius	Acts 17: 15-34	1 31	♎	13	♄ south 8 46	8	7 22	4 38	7 58
Monday	8	Mart. Rinkard	Gen. 15:	2 10	♎	26	♅ south 10 45	8	7 22	4 38	8 46
Tuesday	9	Benj. Schmolk	Deut. 5:	2 59	♏	9	☿ in Perihelion	7	7 23	4 37	9 40
Wednesday	10	Paul Eber	Exodus 12:	3 40	♏	22	☌ ☽ ♀. ♀ rises 3 26	7	7 23	4 37	10 37
Thursday	11	Hen. v. Zutphen	Deut. 27:	4 59	♐	5	☌ ☿ ☉ Inferior	7	7 23	4 37	11 31
Friday	12	Vicelin	Romans 7:	6 10	♐	18	☽ in per. ☌ ☽ ☿	6	7 24	4 36	12 27
Saturday	13	Odilia	Leviticus 16:	☽ sets	♑	0	13th. ♀ in Per. ⌣	6	7 24	4 36	1 22

50] *3d Sunday in Advent,* Matt. 11 : 2–10 ; 1 Cor. 4 : 1–5. *Day's Length,* 9 *hours,* 10 *min.*

Sunday	14	Dioscorus	Is. 40: John 5:	5 44	♑	12	♅ stationary	5	7 25	4 35	2 11
Monday	15	Christiana	1 Pet. 1: 3–12	6 50	♑	24	♅ south 10 24	5	7 25	4 35	3 6
Tuesday	16	Adelheid	2 Samuel 7:	7 46	♒	6	☊. ♅ stationary	4	7 25	4 35	3 46
Wednesday	17	*Ember Day*	Joel 3:	8 49	♒	18	♀ rises 3 34	4	7 25	4 35	4 34
Thursday	18	Louis v. Seckendorf	Jeremiah 23:	9 59	♓	0	☌ ☽ ♃. ♃ sets 10 6	3	7 25	4 35	5 16
Friday	19	Clemens Alexandrinus	" 31:	11 7	♓	12	Sirius rises 7 47	3	7 25	4 35	5 50
Saturday	20	Abraham	Isa. 52: 13–53:	morn.	♓	24	20th. ☿ gr. Hel. Lat. N.	2	7 25	4 35	6 31

51] *4th Sunday in Advent,* John 1 : 19–34 ; Phil. 4 : 4–7. *Day's Length,* 9 *hours,* 8 *min.*

Sunday	21	Thomas	John 3: 23–36	12 14	♈	6	☌ ☽ ♄. ☉ enters ♑ Shortest Day	2	7 26	4 34	7 20
Monday	22	Hugh McKail	Isaiah 42:	1 18	♈	18	Winter commences	1	7 25	4 35	8 12
Tuesday	23	Anna du Bourg	" 49:	2 21	♉	2	♅ south 9 59	1	7 25	4 35	9 6
Wednesday	24	Adam and Eve	" 11: 1–10	3 26	♉	14	☽ in apo. ☌ ☽ ♅	sun	7 25	4 35	9 47
Thursday	25	*Christmas*	Isa. 9: 2-7; Heb. 1	4 39	♉	28	♀ rises 3 38	sl'w	7 25	4 35	10 40
Friday	26	Stephen	Psalm 2: & 110:	5 43	♊	12	♄ south 7 44	1	7 25	4 35	11 35
Saturday	27	St. John Evang.	Isaiah 41:	6 50	♊	27	♃ sets 9 30 ⌒	1	7 25	4 35	12 26

52] *Sunday after Christmas,* Matt. 1 : 18–25 ; Gal. 4 : 1–7. *Day's Length,* 9 *hours,* 10 *min.*

Sunday	28	Innocents	Col. 1:	☽ rise	♋	12	28. Orion so. 11 20	2	7 25	4 35	1 20
Monday	29	David	Rom. 8:	6 30	♋	27	☋. ☿ rises 6 34	2	7 24	4 36	2 11
Tuesday	30	Christ'n of Wurtemburg	1 Cor. 8: 1-6	7 46	♌	12	☿ gr. Elon. West	3	7 24	4 36	2 53
Wednesday	31	John Wiclif	Psa. 90: & 103:	9 1	♌	27	□ ♄ ☉. ☉ in Perigee	3	7 24	4 36	3 42

MOON'S PHASES.

Last Quarter,	6th,	2 o'clock,	45 min.	afternoon.
New Moon,	13th,	6 "	6 "	morning.
First Quarter,	20th,	6 "	14 "	"
Full Moon,	28th,	11 "	13 "	forenoon.

CONJECTURES OF THE WEATHER.

1, 2, cloudy, cold; 3, 4, 5, variable; 6, 7, rain and snow; 8, 9, 10, clear, cold; 11, 12, 13, fair; 14, 15, variable; 16, 17, cloudy; 18, 19, rain; 20, 21, 22, cold; 23, 24, cloudy; 25, 26, variable; 27, 28, snow; 29, 30, 31 cold.

Do you know how beautiful the snow is? Have you ever seen it under a microscope? What lovely stars, diamonds and angles! God sends it, says Job (37 : 6), and all God's works are beautiful.

THE OLD YEAR.

The New Year has become old. All its days have passed away. How solemnly we are admonished, by the close of 1879, to work hard while the day lasts, to pray earnestly for God's blessing upon our work, and patiently to wait for its full fruit.

"Oh, Christians, how the years roll on !
Thousands to their account have gone ;
Our time is short. Work while 'tis day ;
Oh work, and wait, and watch, and pray."

Whatsoever thy hand findeth to do, do it with thy might. There is much for every hand ; and life at longest is short. Every Christian should daily and devoutly say, "I must be about my Father's business."

☞ For the Statistical Summary in this and last year's Almanac, the Editor makes grateful acknowledgment to Rev. I. H. Reiter, D. D. of Miamisburg, O., Stated Clerk of the General Synod.

☞ Those Christians who have so little practice on earth, will hardly know how to go about the Lord's work in heaven.

A CONSTITUTION
FOR AUXILIARY MISSIONARY SOCIETIES.

NAME.

Art. 1. This Society shall be known as the Missionary Society of the Reformed Church and Sunday-school at———————auxiliary to the Board of Missions of the Reformed Church in the United States.

OBJECT.

Art. 2.—The object of this Society shall be to awaken interest in the cause of Missions; to diffuse missionary intelligence, and to secure regular weekly contributions, for the support of missions in the Reformed Church.

OFFICERS.

Art. 3 The officers shall consist of a President, a Vice-President, a Secretary and Treasurer, who shall be elected for the period of one year, and may be re-elected at the option of the Society.

DUTIES OF OFFICERS.

Art. 4. The President, or in his absence the Vice-President, shall preside at all meetings, and attend to such duties as do not interfere with the relations of the pastor as President ex-officio and as hereafter defined.

Art. 5. The Secretary shall keep a correct record of the transactions of the Society, and a roll of the membership.

Art. 6. It shall be the duty of the Treasurer to keep an account of all monies received and disbursed, to pay out all monies as directed by the Society and to make a report to the Society at the end of the year.

MEMBERSHIP.

Art. 7. The members of the Society shall consist of Sunday-school scholars and teachers, members of the Church and friends, who shall contribute at least one cent per week; and each member shall be furnished with a certificate of membership, provided by the Board of Missions, with the name of its officers attached and the seal of the Board.

MEETINGS.

Art. 8. There shall be monthly meetings of this Society either after divine service on Sunday, or at such other times as may be fixed on by resolution of the Society. These meetings, in connection with the transaction of business claiming attention, may be social or devotional as may seem best calculated to promote the object of the Society. At the end of the year a missionary festival shall be held, at which, among other things, the Treasurer's report shall be made, an annual report of the progress and success of the Society shall be read by the President, missionary addresses delivered, and such other exercises observed, as wi'l tend to promote the cause of missions in the congregations.

FUNDS.

Art. 9. The funds of this Society shall be paid over to the Treasurer of the Board of Missions, established by the three Synods of the Reformed Church, the Synod of the United States, the Pittsburgh Synod, and the Synod of the Potomac.

STANDING COMMITTEE.

Art. 10. A Standing Committee, of which the officers of the Society shall be members, shall consist of ten persons, who shall be elected annually by the Society. It shall be the duty of this committee, to interest the Society in the work of missions, to secure the names of new members, and to carry out any instructions which may be given by the Society.

THE DUTIES OF THE PASTOR.

Art. 11. The pastor shall be President ex-officio, preside at the meetings of the Society, whenever he shall deem it necessary; conduct all religious services, and in his absence appoint some one for that purpose, assist the members by his counsel, and endeavor to secure the co-operation of the members of the congregation.

BY-LAWS.

Art. 12. By-Laws can be adopted by this Society to meet any wants which have not herein been provided for.

ANNUAL MEETINGS OF THE VIRGINIA CLASSIS.

The Virginia Classis was organized at Woodstock, Shenandoah County, Virginia, May 30th, 1825, and met annually until May 16th, 1829, when they failed of a Constitutional quorum, and the Classis was dissolved.

The Classis was re-organized at Woodstock, Shenandoah County, Virginia, November 14th, 1839. Rev. J. Heller, President, and Rev. Wm. F. Colliflower, Secretary. Rev. Wm. F. Colliflower was elected Secretary in 1840, and Rev. Jeremiah Heller in 1841. Rev. J. C. Hensell served as Stated Clerk from 1842 to 1848. Rev. H. St. John Rinker has held the offices of Stated Clerk and Treasurer from 1848 to the present.

	PLACE.	TIME.	PRESIDENT.
1st.	Friedens Church, Rockingham Co... Va.	May 14th, 1840	Rev. J. C. Hensell.
2d.	Winchester, Frederick Co.............. "	" 9th, 1841......	" J. C. Hensell.
3d.	St. John's Church, Augusta Co....... "	" 14th, 1842......	" Daniel Feete.
4th.	Grace Church, Page Co............. ..... "	" 20th, 1843......	" D. G. Bragonier.
5th.	Zion's Church, Shenandoah Co....... "	" 18th, 1844......	" G. H. Martin.
6th.	McGaheysville, Rockingham Co...... "	" 17th, 1845......	" J. W. Hoffmier.
7th.	Lovettsville, Loudon Co...-........... "	" 16th, 1846......	" H. St. J. Rinker.
8th.	Newport, Augusta Co.......... . ... "	" 15th, 1847......	" Daniel Feete.
9th.	Smithfield, Jefferson Co............... "	" 20th, 1848......	" Geo. W. Williard.
10th.	Mount Crawford, Rockingham Co... "	" 19th, 1849......	" S. J. Fetzer.
11th.	Zion's Church, Pendleton Co......... "	" 18th, 1850......	" Daniel Feete.
12th.	Union Forge, Shenandoah Co........ "	" 17th, 1851......	" G. H. Martin.
13th.	Shepherdstown, Jefferson Co........ "	" 14th, 1852......	" D. G. Bragonier.
14th.	St. John's Church, Augusta Co....... "	" 15th, 1853......	" J. C. Hensell.
15th.	Zion's Church, Shenandoah Co...... "	" 18th, 1854......	" Daniel Feete.
16th.	Smithfield, Jefferson Co............... "	" 17th, 1855......	" G. H. Martin.
17th.	Woodstock, Shenandoah Co.......... "	" 16th, 1856......	" J. C. Hensell.
18th.	Lovettsville, Loudon Co.............. "	" 15th, 1857......	" D. G. Bragonier.
19th.	Edinburg, Shenandoah Co............ "	" 14th, 1858......	" G. H. Martin.
20th.	Mt. Crawford, Rockingham Co....... "	" 13th, 1859......	" J. H. Crawford.
21st.	Middlebrook, Augusta Co............. "	" 18th, 1860......	" J. C. Hensell.
22d.	Woodstock, Shenandoah Co.......... "	Sept. 21st, 1861......	" D. G. Bragonier.
23d.	Woodstock, Shenandoah Co.......... "	May 18th, 1866*.....	" G. H. Martin.
24th.	Shepherdstown, Jefferson Co........ W. Va.	" 18th, 1867......	" H. Wissler.
25th.	Edinburg, Shenandoah Co............ Va.	" 15th, 1868......	" J. C. Hensell.
26th.	Rockland Mills, Augusta Co......... "	" 14th, 1869......	" W. D. Lefever.
27th.	Martinsburg, Berkley Co............ W. Va.	" 18th, 1870......	" M. L. Shuford.
28th.	Woodstock, Shenandoah Co.......... Va.	" 17th, 1871......	" John Lantz.
29th.	Mt. Crawford, Rockingham Co...... "	" 15th, 1872......	" G. H. Martin.
30th.	Winchester, Frederick Co............ "	" 14th, 1873......	" J. C. Hensell.
31st.	St. John's Church, Augusta Co...... "	" 15th, 1874......	" S. N. Callender, D. D.
32d.	Shepherdstown, Jefferson Co........ W. Va.	April 15th, 1875......	" G. H. Martin.
33d.	Grace Church, Shenandoah Co...... Va.	May 18th, 1876......	" C. G. Fisher.
34th.	Lovettsville, Loudon Co............. ..... "	" 17th, 1877	" J. S. Loose.
35th.	St. Michael's Ch., Rockingham Co... "	" 31st, 1878......	" J. S. Loose.

* Owing to the Civil War Classis failed to meet from 1862 to 1865 inclusive.

Lovettsville, Loudon Co., Va.   J. F. RINKER.

ORPHAN HOMES OF THE REFORMED CHURCH IN THE UNITED STATES.

LOCATION.	SUPERINTENDENT.	NUMBER OF ORPHANS.
Womelsdorf, Berks County, Pa...............	Rev. D. B. Albright...............................	54
Butler, Butler County, Pa.....................,....	Rev. T. F. Stauffer.............................	35

CHURCH TREASURERS.

GENERAL SYNOD.

Treasurer.—WM. D. GROSS, 3809 Haverford St., Phila., Pa.

Treasurer of Home Missions.—CHARLES SANTEE, 239 N. Third St., Philadelphia.

Treasurer of Church Extension.—GEORGE GELBACH, 1701 Master St., Philadelphia.

Treasurer of Foreign Missions.—HON. R. F. KELKER, Harrisburg, Pa.

Treasurer of Society for the Relief of Ministers.—Rev. THEODORE APPEL, D. D., Lancaster, Pa.

SYNOD OF THE UNITED STATES.

Treasurer.—GEORGE W. HENSEL, Lancaster, Pa.

Treasurer of Board of Education.—Rev. Dr. SAMUEL R. FISHER, 907 Arch St., Philadelphia.

SYNOD OF PITTSBURGH.

Treasurer.—T. J. CRAIG, Pittsburgh, Pa.

Treasurer of Board of Education.—Rev. Dr. GEO. B. RUSSELL, 1444 N St., N. W., Washington, D. C.

SYNOD OF THE POTOMAC.

Treasurer.—LOUIS MARKEL, Frederick, Md.

Treasurer of Board of Education.—Rev. W. M. DEATRICK, Mercersburg, Franklin County, Pa.

BOARD OF HOME MISSIONS OF THE JOINT SYNODS.

Treasurer.—WM. H. SEIBERT, Harrisburg, Pa.

Superintendent of Missions.—Rev. THEODORE APPEL, D. D., Lancaster, Pa.

GERMAN SYNOD OF THE EAST.

Treasurer.—CONRAD BREIDENBACH, 1102 Ridge Avenue, Philadelphia, Pa.

Treasurer of Missions.—W. D. GROSS, 3809 Haverford St., Philadelphia, Pa.

SYNOD OF OHIO.

Treasurer.—Rev. J. H. GOOD, D. D., Tiffin, O.

Treasurer of Board of Education.—Rev. REUBEN GOOD, Tiffin, O.

Treasurer of Home Missions.—Rev. L. H. KEFAUVER, Tiffin, O.

SYNOD OF THE NORTHWEST.

Treasurer.—Rev. F. FORWICK, 105 Fulton St., Cleveland, O.

Treasurer of Missions.—Rev. DAN'L ZIMMERMAN, Galion, O.

THEOLOGICAL SEMINARY, LANCASTER, PA.

Treasurer.—JOHN B. ROTH, Lancaster, Pa.

THEOLOGICAL SEMINARY, TIFFIN, O.

Treasurer.—Rev. I. H. REITER, D. D., Miamisburg, O.

FRANKLIN AND MARSHALL COLLEGE.

Treasurer.—JACOB DAUSMAN, Lancaster, Pa.

HEIDELBERG COLLEGE, TIFFIN, O.

Treasurer.—Hon. N. L. BREWER, Tiffin, O.

MERCERSBURG COLLEGE.

Treasurer.—ADAM B. WINGERD, Greencastle, Pa.

URSINUS COLLEGE.

Treasurer.—FRANK M. HOBSON, Freeland, Montgomery Co., Penna.

MISSION HOUSE, SHEBOYGAN, WIS.

Treasurer.—Rev. JOHN F. KLUGE, Sheboygan, Wis.

BETHANY ORPHANS' HOME, WOMELSDORF, PA.

Treasurer.—WM. D. GROSS, 3809 Haverford St., Phila., Pa.

ST. PAUL'S ORPHANS' HOME, BUTLER, PA.

Treasurer.—B. WOLFF, JR., Craig St., Pittsburgh, Pa.

STATISTICAL SUMMARY OF THE REFORMED CHURCH IN THE UNITED STATES.

SYNODS.	Classes.	Ministers.	Congregations.	Members.	Members Unconfirmed.	BAPTISMS. Infants.	Adults.	ADDITIONS. Confirmed.	By Certificate.	Communed.	Dismissed.	Excommunicated.	Erasure of Names.	Deaths.	Sunday-schools.	Sunday-school Scholars.	Students for the Ministry.	CONTRIBUTIONS. Benevolent Purposes.	Congregational Purposes.
Synod of U. S........	8	204	430	63,081	37,221	5,357	219	3,623	1,147	50,623	559	13		2 353	468	33,730	67	$22,782	$200,717
Synod of Ohio.......	12	162	340	24,560	11,307	1,496	464	1,607	737	19,592	268	19	403	541	253	20,134	23	7,032	80,870
Synod of N. W.......	9	132	202	16,459	13,048	1,627	9	989	762	13,185	230	111	11	482	164	9,692	18	7,980	58,032
Synod of Pittsburg..	5	52	114	9,722	7,536	702	23	500	203	8,473	156	1	46	223	96	5,680	14	5,816	54,000
Synod of Potomac..	6	122	247	26,230	16,223	1,621	143	1,200	456	22,085	290	2		721	215	15,175	31	13,923	85,624
Ger. Synod of East..	5	38	36	7,736	5,655	1,520	22	537	411	6,723	63	28	52	567	37	5,571	4	4,194	52,986
Total : 6 Synods......	45	710	1,369	147,788	90,993	12,323	880	8,456	3,716	120,681	1,566	174	512	4,887	1,237	89,982	157	$61,727	$532,229

SYNOD OF OHIO.

I. BOARD OF HOME MISSIONS.

OFFICERS.

Rev. THEODORE J. BACHER, *President*, Wooster, Ohio.
" JOHN J. LEBERMAN, *Sec'y and Treas.*, Louisville, Ohio.

MEMBERS.

Rev. JOHN M. KENDIG,   Rev. THEODORE H. BACHER,
" JOHN J. LEBERMAN,   " HENRY HILBISH,
     Elder ROBERT BELL.

II. BOARD OF CHURCH ERECTION.

OFFICERS.

Rev. PETER C. PRUGH, *President*, Germantown, O.
" SAMUEL B. YOCKEY, *Secretary*, Xenia, O.
" ISAAC H. REITER, D. D., *Treasurer*, Miamisburg, O.

MEMBERS.

Rev. ISAAC H. REITER, D.D.,   Rev. PETER C. PRUGH,
" SAMUEL B. YOCKEY,   " HENRY M. HERMAN.
     Elder BENJAMIN KUHNS.

BOARDS OF MISSIONS OF GENERAL SYNOD.

I. BOARD OF HOME MISSIONS.

OFFICERS.

Rev. JACOB O. MILLER, D. D., *President*, York, Pa.
" JOHN A. PETERS, *Secretary*, Alexandria, Pa.
Elder CHARLES SANTEE, *Treasurer*, Philadelphia, Pa.

MEMBERS.

Rev. JACOB O. MILLER, D.D.   Rev. JOHN KUELLING, D.D.
" GEO. B. RUSSELL, D.D.   " C. R. DIEFFENBACHER.
" GEO. H. JOHNSTON.   Elder CHARLES SANTEE.
" WM. H. H. SNYDER.   " WILLIAM D. GROSS.
" JOHN A. PETERS.   " DANIEL W. GROSS.
" JOHN M. TITZEL.   " CHRISTIAN M. BOUSII.

II. BOARD OF FOREIGN MISSIONS.

OFFICERS.

Rev. DAVID VAN HORNE, D. D., *President*, Philadelphia, Pa.
" CHAS. H. LEINBACH, D.D., *Vice-Pres.*, Stouchsburg, Pa.
" THOS. S. JOHNSTON, D.D., *Secretary*, Lebanon, Pa.
" CLEM. Z. WEISER, D. D., *Cor. Sec.*, East Greenville, Pa.
Hon. RUDOLPH F. KELKER, *Treasurer*, Harrisburg, Pa.

MEMBERS.

Rev. THOS. S. JOHNSTON, D.D.   Rev. CLEM. Z. WEISER, D.D.
" BENJ. BAUSMAN, D.D.   " D. VAN HORNE, D.D.
" NICHOLAS GEHR, D.D.   Elder G. S. GRIFFITH.
" J. H. A. BOMBERGER, D.D.   " RUDOLPH F. KELKER.
" JOSEPH W. SANTEE, D.D.   " WM. H. SEIBERT.
" CHAS. H. LEINBACH, D.D.   " GEORGE GELBACH.

III. BOARD OF DIRECTORS OF ORPHAN HOMES.

Rev. JACOB DAHLMAN and Elder WILLIAM E. SCHMERTZ elected in 1872.
" GEO. B. RUSSELL, D. D., and Elder WILLIAM D. GROSS "   1875.
WILLIAM F. HOFFMAN, M. D.,   "   1878.

LITERARY AND THEOLOGICAL INSTITUTIONS OF THE REFORMED CHURCH IN THE U. S.

NAME.	LOCATION.	PRESIDENTS.
Franklin and Marshall College	Lancaster, Pa.	T. G. APPLE, D. D.
Heidelberg College	Tiffin, Ohio	GEO. W. WILLIARD, D. D.
Catawba College	Newton, N. C.	Rev. J. C. CLAPP, A. M.
Mercersburg College	Mercersburg, Pa.	E. E. HIGBEE, D. D.
Clarion Collegiate Institute	Rimersburg, Clarion Co., Pa.	Rev. J. J. PENNYPACKER, D. D.
Palatinate College	Meyerstown, Lebanon Co., Pa.	G. W. AUGHINBAUGH, D. D.
Juniata Collegiate Institute	Martinsburg, Blair Co., Pa.	P. H. BRIDENBAUGH, A. B.
Greensburg Female Collegiate Institute	Greensburg, Pa.	Rev. LUCIAN CORT, A. M.
Ursinus College	Collegeville, Montgomery Co., Pa.	J. H. A. BOMBERGER, D. D.
Calvin Institute	Cleveland, Ohio	Rev. A. ACCOLA.
Eastern Theological Seminary	Lancaster, Pa.	E. V. GERHART, D. D.
Western Theological Seminary	Tiffin, Ohio	J. H. GOOD, D. D.
Mission House	Howard's Grove, Wisconsin.	J. BOSSARD, D. D.
Allentown Female College	Allentown, Pa.	Rev. W. R. HOFFORD, A. M.
St. John's Select School	Knoxville, Md.	G. L. STALEY, D. D.
Female Seminary	Mercersburg, Pa.	Rev. J. HASSLER, A. M.

MEETING OF THE CLASSES

OF THE SYNOD OF THE UNITED STATES, THE SYNOD OF PITTSBURGH, AND THE SYNOD OF THE POTOMAC.

CLASSES.	PLACE.	TIME.
EAST PENNSYLVANIA..	Lehighton, Carbon Co., Pa..........	May 19th, 1879........
LEBANON...	Womelsdorf, Berks Co., Pa..................................	June 5th, 1879.......
PHILADELPHIA...........	Church of the Ascension, Norristown, Pa.................	June 6th, 1879........
LANCASTER...	Litiz, Lancaster Co., Pa.......	June 5th, 1879........
EAST SUSQUEHANNA	Turbotville, Northumberland Co., Pa....................	June 5th, 1879........
WEST SUSQUEHANNA................................	Bellefonte, Centre Co., Pa.................................	May 21st, 1879.......
GOSHENHOPPEN....................	Wentz Church, Montgomery Co., Pa.	May 30th, 1879........
TOHICKON................................	Ridge Valley, Bucks Co., Pa..............................	June 2d, 1879.......
WESTMORELAND......................................	Manor Church, Westmoreland Co., Pa...................	May 30th, 1879.......
CLARION.......................................	Kittanning, Armstrong Co., Pa................................	June 5th, 1879........
ST. PAUL'S..........	St. John's Church, Shenango Charge, Mercer Co., Pa..	June 5th, 1879........
SOMERSET...	Salem Church, Frostburg, Md..........................	June 4th, 1879.......
ALLEGHENY..	Grace Church, Pittsburgh, Pa................................	May 28th, 1879.......
ZION'S...	St. Jacob's Church, Emanuel's Charge, York Co., Pa...	May 16th, 1879.......
MARYLAND.................................	Jefferson, Frederick Co., Md...............................	May 15th, 1879........
MERCERSBURG...	Shippensburg, Cumberland Co., Pa...................	May 14th, 1879.......
VIRGINIA..	Smithfield, Jefferson Co., Va................................	May 15th, 1879........
NORTH CAROLINA..................................	Emanuel's Church, Davidson Co., N. C..............	May 22d, 1879.......
SAN FRANCISCO..........	....	....

PERIODICALS OF THE REFORMED CHURCH IN THE U. S.

NAME.	WHERE PUBLISHED.	HOW OFTEN ISSUED.	WHEN FIRST ISSUED.
English.—			
The Messenger..........................	907 Arch Street, Philadelphia, Pa........	Weekly..............	.... 1827........
Christian World.......................	Dayton, Ohio	"	.... 1848............
The Guardian.........................	907 Arch Street, Philadelphia, Pa.........	Monthly......................	.... 1850........
Child's Treasury.........................	" " " "	Semi-monthly..........	.... 1859........
Mercersburg Review..................	" " " "	Quarterly...............	.... 1849........
The Instructor.........................	Dayton Ohio......................	Monthly.................	.... 1873........
Leaves of Light	" "	Semi-monthly..........	... . 1873........
College Days..........................	Lancaster, Pa...............................	Monthly...............	.... 1873........
German.—			
Kirchenzeitung and Evangelist.....	Cleveland, Ohio..................................	Weekly...............	.... 1838........
Reformirte Hausfreund..............	Reading, Pa..................................	Every other week..	.... 1866........
Der Lammerhirte.....................	Cleveland, Ohio...................................	Monthly..................	.... 1859........

DEATHS OF MINISTERS FROM SEPTEMBER 1st, 1877 TO SEPTEMBER 1st, 1878.

NAMES.	LICENSED.	ORDAINED.	PLACE OF DEATH.	TIME OF DEATH.	AGE.
BENJAMIN SCHNEIDER, D. D.......	Spring of 1833..	October, 1833..	Boston, Mass.................	Sept. 14, 1877....	70
JOHN ADAM LEIS.....................	June 7, 1835..	June 7, 1835..	Wernersville, Pa.............	Oct. 28, 1877....	71
JOHN G. WOLFF.....................	Sept., 1836..	Jan. 12, 1837..	Lancaster, Pa.................	Jan. 22, 1878....	67
C. Plüss...........................	Emigrated from	Germany 1849..	Crothersville, Ind..........	Feb. 28, 1878....	53
HERMAN BOKUM.....................	October, 1842..	Dec. 5, 1843..	Germantown, Pa.............	Aug. 5, 1878....	72
NICHOLAS P. HACKE, D. D.........	Sept. 9, 1819..	Sept. 9, 1819..	Greensburg, Pa...............	Aug. 25, 1878....	78

ALPHABETICAL REGISTER OF THE MINISTERS OF THE REFORMED CHURCH OF THE U. S.

Accola, O. J., Dayton, Ohio.
Addams, Geo. K., Mifflinburg, Union Co., Pa.
Albright, D. R., Womelsdorf, Berks Co., Pa.
Albright, Geo. H., Brandon, Buchanan Co., Iowa.
Albright, G. M., New Lisbon, Columbiana Co., O.
Alepach, J. W., Barnhart Mills, Butler Co., Pa.
Andrews, W. M., Reedsburg, Ohio.
Appel, Dr. Theodore, Lancaster, Pa.
Appel, R. S., Hamburg, Berks Co., Pa.
Apple, J. H., Saegertown, Crawford Co., Pa.
Apple, Dr. T. G., Prof., Lancaster, Pa.
Anghinbaugh, Dr. G.W., Meyerstown, Leb. Co., Pa
Ault, John, Littlestown, Adams Co., Pa.

Bacher, T. J., Wooster, Ohio.
Bachman, Adam J., Schaefferstown, Leb. Co., Pa.
Bachman, James N., Jacksonville, Lehigh Co., Pa
Bechman, John, Cincinnati, Ohio.
Beckman, M., 127 Bank st., Baltimore, Md.
Badertscher, C., Giard, Clayton Co., Iowa.
Bahner, F. F., Waynesboro', Franklin Co., Pa.
Balchley, A.K.C., Liberty Centre, Henry Co., Ohio.
Bair, H., North Washington, Westmorel'd Co., Pa.
Bank, G., New Brunswick, N. J.
Barbar, J. W., Bremen, Fairfield Co., Ohio.
Barkley, T. J., 81 Fayette st., Allegheny City, Pa.
Barth, Sebastian, 377 N.W. St., Indianapolis, Ind.
Bartholomew, A. R., Jonestown, Lebanon Co., Pa.
Bartholomew, A., Lehighton, Carbon Co., Pa.
Basslar, H. S., Millersburg, Dauphin Co., Pa.
Bates, W. H., Stoystown, Somerset Co., Pa.
Baum, O., Pottsville, Schuylkill Co., Pa.
Bauman, R., Abilene, Dickinson Co., Kansas.
Bauman, F. G., Zwingli, Dubuque Co., Iowa.
Bausman, Dr. B., Reading, Pa.
Beade, J. C., Sidney, Ohio.
Beam, S. Z., Mt. Pleasant, Westmoreland Co., Pa.
Beck, Charles, Wakarusa, Ind.
Beck, John H., Lake, Stark Co., Ohio.
Becker, Augustus, Waukegan, Ill.
Becker, Charles, 676 N. 46th st., Phila.
Becker, Chas., Broadheadville, Monroe Co., Pa.
Becker, Cyrus J., Catasauqua, Lehigh Co., Pa.
Becker, Philip, Mt. Eaton, Wayne Co., Ohio.
Beisser, G., Decatur, Adams Co., Ind.
Bentz, H., Clarence, Erie Co., N. Y.
Berents, C., Grandview, Ohio.
Berleman, F. W., Louisville, Ky.
Beyer, G. E. W., Grand Junction, Greene Co., Iowa.
Bielfeld, Herman, Frederick, Md.
Biery, Benj. F. Cornfield, Lehigh Co., Pa.
Biery, John, Walholding, Coshocton Co., Ohio.
Bistgen, J., Northelm, Manitowoc Co., Wis.
Boerchers, C., Baltimore, Md.
Boley, Adam, 710 Selfridge st., Philadelphia, Pa.
Bolliger, A., Hiawatha, Brown Co., Kansas.
Bombergar, Dr. J. H. A., College's, Mont. Co., Pa.
Bonekemper, W., Sutton, Clay Co., Nebraska.
Boward, Dr. Jacob, Franklin, Sheboygan Co., Wis.
Bowers, A. J., Weyer's Cave, Augusta Co., Va.

Bowman, John C., Shepherdst'n, Jeff. Co., W. Va.
Braun, J. R., Vermillion, Erie Co., Ohio.
Braun, William, 84 Hague st., Cleveland, Ohio.
Brecht, J. J., Sank City, Sank Co., Wis.
Braidenbach, S. R., Berlin, Somerset Co., Pa.
Brendle, D. F., Bethlehem, Pa.
Brown, I. G., Mercersburg, Pa.
Brüngger, H., Kohlville, Washington Co., Wis.
Brunner, K., Bridgeport, Conn.
Bucher, Dr. John C., Lewisburg, Union Co., Pa.
Bushe, John F., 108 Rivington st., New York.
Buser, J. H., Cone, Muscatine Co., Iowa.
Butt, A., Montpelier, Ohio.
Butler, Joseph F., Collegeville, Montg'y Co., Pa.
Callender, Dr. S. N., Pleasant Valley, Rockingham Co., Va.
Carnahan, D.R., Mt. Jackson, Shenandoah Co., Va.
Caspar, A. B., New Berlin, Union Co., Pa.
Casselman, Amos, Fostoria, O.
Cast, Charles, Egg Harbor City, N. J.
Cecil, J. W., Thomasville, Davidson Co., N. C.
Clapp, Prof. J. C., Newton, N. C.
Clauser, W. W., White Deer Mills, Union Co., Pa.
Clemens, John M., Conyngham, Luzerne Co., Pa.
Clever, Conrad, Columbia, Pa.
Colliflower, Wm. F., New Oxford, Adams Co., Pa.
Comfort, H. H., Chambersburg, Pa.
Cook, H. E., Hagerstown, Md.
Coon, Charles H., Hagerstown, Md.
Cort, Cyrus, Maquoketa, Jackson Co., Iowa.
Cort, Lucian, Greensburg, Westmorel'd Co., Pa.
Crawford, James, Lewisburg, Union Co., Pa.
Cremer, W. C., Chambersburg, Pa.
Crist, J. J., Catasauqua, Lehigh Co., Pa.
Cristloe, F. F., Germano, Harrison Co., Ohio.

Dahlman, A. K., 236 S. 5th st., Brooklyn, E. D., N. Y.
Dahlman, Jacob, 213 N. 39th st., Phila., Pa.
Daniel, H., Nazareth, Northampton Co., Pa.
Darbaker, Harry D., East End, Pittsburgh, Pa.
Davis, Dr. P. S., 907 Arch st., Phila., Pa.
Davis, W. F. P., Reading, Berks Co., Pa.
Deatrich, W. R. H., Mechanicsb'g, Cumb. Co., Pa.
Deatrick, Wm. M., Mercersb'g, Franklin Co., Pa.
Dechant, A. L., Pennsbury, Mont. Co., Pa.
Dechant, F. W., Reading, Pa.
Dechant, G. B., Catawissa, Columbia Co., Pa.
De Long, J. F., Williamsport, Pa.
Dengler, J. G., Sellersville, Bucks Co., Pa.
Denny, J. C., Gold Hill, Rowan Co., N. C.
Derr, J. H., Henry, Marshall Co., Ill.
Derr, L. K., Slatington, Lehigh Co., Pa.
Derr, Tilghman, Berwick, Columbia Co., Pa.
Detrich, J. D., Flowertown, Montgomery Co., Pa.
Dieckman, William, New Bremen, Ohio.
Dieckmann, Frederick, Lock-box W., Wheatland, Iowa.
Dieckmann, J. F. H., Louisville, Ky.
Dieffenbacher, C. B., Greensb'g, Westm'd Co., Pa.

Dieffenbacher, D. S., Kittanning, Pa.
Dieffenbacher, E. H., Wyoming, Kent Co., Del.
Diefenderfer, M. H., Eikerton, Armstr'g Co., Pa.
Diether, F., Allegheny City, Pa.
Dietz, T. R., Sprankle's Mills, Jefferson Co., Pa.
Dingledine, J. E., Bradford, Ohio.
Dippel, Peter H., Huntington, Ind.
Dittmar, D. N., St. Clairsville, Bedford Co., Pa.
Dole, A. G., Huntingdon, Pa.
Donat, Willoughby, Oriental, Juniata Co., Pa.
Dotterer, J., New Berlin, Union Co., Pa.
Dubbs, A. J. G., Allentown, Pa.
Dubbs, Dr. J. H., Prof., Lancaster, Pa.
Duenger, R., Fountain Spring, Schuylkill Co., Pa.

Ebbert, D. W., Shippensburg, Cumberl'd Co., Pa.
Ebbinghaus, J. W., Washington, D. C.
Edmonds, F. A., Harmony, Butler Co., Pa.
Edmonds, L. C., Emporia, Lyon Co., Kan.
Eichen, J., Linton, Green Co., Ind.
Ellicker, Sol., Baxter, Jasper Co., Iowa.
Engle, W. G., Pillow, Dauphin Co., Pa.
Epstein, Eph. M., Tiffin, O.
Erb, Edmond, Apple Creek, Ohio.
Eschbach, Dr. E. R., Frederick, Md.
Eselborn, O., Loran, Stephenson Co., Ill.
Evans, L., Kryder, Pottstown, Pa.
Evans, John M., Penn Hall, Centre Co., Pa.

Facius, Gustav., Baltimore, Md.
Falk, Theodore, Omaha, Nebraska.
Feete, Daniel, Norristown, Pa.
Feige, W., Marengo, Iowa Co., Iowa.
Fenneman, W. H., Waterloo, Indiana.
Ferer, Benjamin D., Easton, Pa.
Fisher, Charles G., Winchester, Va.
Fisher, Dr. S. R., 907 Arch st., Phila., Pa.
Fienner, L., Jeffersonville, Indiana.
Fogel, Edward J., Fogelsville, Lehigh Co., Pa.
Foil, J. A., Newton, Catawba Co., N. C.
Forwix, F., 105 Platoa st., Cleveland, Ohio.
Fouse, D. S., Lisbon, Linn Co., Iowa.
Fox, F., Harrisburg, Pa.
Frank, Milton F., Farmersville, Ohio.
Freeman, Jos. K., Waisport, Carbon Co., Pa.
Friebolin, W., Owatonna, Steele Co., Minn.
Fritchey, J. G., Lancaster, Pa.
Fritsch, M. L., Reading, Pa.
Fritzinger, J., Allentown, Lehigh Co., Pa.
Foundeling, Julius, San Francisco, Cal.
Fulcason, D. K., Blue Mound, Illinois.
Fuerer, E. F. E., Alma, Buffalo Co., Wis.

Gans, Dr. D., No. 67 N. Paca st., Baltimore, Md.
Gansen, R., Huron, Ohio.
Gantenbein, J., Portland, Oregon.
Garner, H. S., Schellsburg, Bedford Co., Pa.
Gast, Dr. F. A., Prof., Lancaster, Pa.
Geary, A. C., Keedysville, Washington Co., Md.
Gehr, Dr. N., 1230 N. Sixth st., Phila., Pa.
Geimel, J. F., Columbia City, Indiana.

Gerhard, Calvin J., Sunbury, Pa.
Gerhard, D. W., New Holland, Lanc'r Co., Pa.
Gerberd, W. T., Lancaster, Pa.
Gerhart, Dr. E. V., Prof., Lancaster, Pa.
Gerhart, Henry L., East Greenville, Mont. Co., Pa.
Gerhart, R. L., Riegelsville, Bucks Co., Pa.
Gilda, N. E , Mechanicstown, Fred. Co., Md.
Gilpin, Wm., Basil, Fairfield Co., Ohio.
Glessner, Dr. G.W., Shippensburg, Cum'd Co., Pa.
Good, Charles W., Shelby, Ohio.
Good, Dr. J. H., Prof., Tiffin, Ohio.
Good, James I., 1525 N. 10th st., Phila., Pa.
Good, R., Prof., Tiffin, Ohio.
Goodrich, W., Clearspring, Wash. Co., Md.
Goss, Sebastian C., Wadsworth, Medina Co., O.
Graeff, I. E., Tamaqua, Schuylkill Co., Pa.
Graf, J. F., Monticello, Iowa.
Grant, Jas., Bradenville, Westmoreland Co., Pa.
Grauel, Julius, Boka, Huston Co., Minn.
Greding, Dr. P., New Philadelphia, Ohio.
Greenawald, Daniel J., Sabetha, Brown Co., Kan.
Greiss, Fred., Darnsburg, Hamilton Co., O.
Grether, J. M., Canton, Stark Co., Ohio.
Gring, Ambrose D., Shrewsbury, York Co., Pa.
Gring, D., Shrewsbury, York Co., Pa.
Gring, John, Fredericksburg, Leb. Co., Pa.
Gring, W. A., Buffalo Mills, Bedford Co., Pa.
Grivelly, J., Boone, Boone Co., Iowa.
Groh, William H., Boalsburg, Centre Co., Pa.
Groh, Milton H., Lake, Ohio.
Grosenbaugh, L., Three Rivers, Mich.
Gross, S. K., Zellersville, Bucks Co., Pa.
Grosshosch, T., Dundee, Richland Co., Ill.
Groeningen, J. G., Sauk City, Wis.
Grünstein, E. K., Linton, Ind.
Guenther, A., St. Kilian, Fon du Lac Co., Wis.
Gundlach, C., Rochester, N. Y.
Gurley, G. D., Latrobe, Westmoreland Co., Pa.

Haas, W. A., Selinsgrove, Snyder Co., Pa.
Hackman, W. C., Burr Oak, Mich.
Hahn, F. D., Greenville, Mercer Co., Pa.
Hale, James T., New Lisbon, Columbiana Co., O.
Hole, W. A., Dayton, Montgomery Co., O.
Hanhart, H., 69 Milton st., Cincinnati, Ohio.
Hannaberry, J., Baldwin, Butler Co., Pa.
Hansen, W., 214 Russell st., Detroit, Mich.
Hartman, Charles, Charleston, Clark Co., Ind.
Hartman, John, Tamaqua, Schuylkill Co., Pa.
Harimetz, Fred. P., Sharon, Mercer Co., Pa.
Hartzell, J. M., Chalfant, Bucks Co., Pa.
Hassler, J., Mercersburg, Franklin Co., Pa.
Hauser, J. Conrad, 107 N. Schroeder st., Balt., Md.
Hauser, Jacob, Mowl, Wis.
Hawker, Adam, Dayton, Ohio.
Headrick, M. L., Lexington, N. C.
Heberle, J., Pittsburgh, Pa.
Heckmann, J., 601 Sycamore st., Cincinnati, O.
Heffley, J., Canal Winchester, Ohio.
Heilman, Calvin U., Elk Lick, Som. Co., Pa.
Heilman, U. H., Duncannon, Perry Co., Pa.

Heinemann, Arnold, Defiance, Defiance Co., O.
Heinze, Moritz, Delphos, Allen Co., Ohio.
Heisler, Dan. Y., Easton, Northampton Co., Pa.
Helfrich, Dr. W. A., Fogelsville, Lehigh Co., Pa.
Heller, A. J., Arendtsville, Adams Co., Pa.
Helming, H., 83 N. Alabama st., Ind'napolis, Ind.
Hendrickson, W. C., Bristol, Bucks Co., Pa.
Henneman, J. C., Beaver, Pike Co., Ohio.
Henning, G. W., Canton, Ohio.
Henry, Austin, Hallsville, Ohio.
Henry, Jerome D., Plymouth, Indiana.
Henschens, C.W.,Manitowoc, Outagamie Co.,Wis.
Honsell, J. C., Mt. Crawford, Va.
Herbert, H. W., Landisburg, Perry Co., Pa.
Herbruck, Edward, Canton, Ohio.
Herbruck, Dr. P., Canton, Ohio.
Herbruck, Emil P., Akron, Ohio.
Herman, A. J., Maxatawny, Berks Co., Pa.
Herman, H. M., W. Alexandria, Preble Co., O.
Herman, J. S., Kutztown, Berks Co., Pa.
Harman, L. C., Pottstown, Montgomery Co., Pa.
Herold, Julius, Akron, Ohio.
Herr, Wm., Prospect, Marion Co., Ohio.
Hershey, Scott F., Denver, Ind.
Hertzell, G. P., Walker, Centre Co., Pa.
Heusser, H., Fountain City, Buffalo Co., Wis.
Hayser, H. C., Rochester, N. Y.   [ton Co., Pa.
Hibschman, H. H. W., Stone Church, Northamp-
Hiester, Eli, Friedensburg, Schuylkill Co., Pa.
Hiester, Dr. J. E., Annville, Lebanon Co., Pa.
Higbee, Dr. E. E., Prof., Mercersburg, Pa.
Hilbish, Henry, North Lima, Mahoning Co., O.
Hines, Jesse, Akron, Ohio.
Hinske, E. R., 1189 State st., Chicago, Ill.
Hoffheins, John A., Martinsburg, Berkley Co.,
    West Virginia.
Hoffman, H., Monroe, Clarion Co., Pa.
Hoffman, P. P. A., Oley, Berks Co., Pa.
Hoffmeier, H. W., Lancaster, Pa.
Hoffmeier, T. F., Middletown, Frederick Co., Md.
Hofford, W. H., Allentown, Pa.
Horstmeyer, W. H., Millville, Butler Co., Ohio.
Hottenstein, A. R., Greenbrier, Northumberland
    Co., Pa.
Houpt, Wm. C., Lineville, Clarion Co., Pa.
Houtz, Alfred, Orangeville, Columbia Co., Pa.
Hoyman, C. W., Somerset, Ohio.
Huber, S. M. K., Worcester, Mont. Co., Pa.
Huber, T. A., Broadheadville, Monroe Co., Pa.
Huecker, H. F., Covington, Ky.
Huecker, John C., Elmore, Fon du Lac Co., Wis.
Huilhorst, F. J. A., Columbus, Nebraska.
Huilhorst, F., Headland, Saunders Co., Neb.
Hunsche, F., Black Creek, Holmes Co., O.
Hustedt, C. F. W., Leslie, Van Wert Co., Ohio.

Ihle, Jacob, Baltimore, Ohio.
Ingle, J., Shaw's Mills, Guilford Co., N. C.
Ingold, Jer., Hickory Tavern, Catawba Co., N. C.

Jannett, John J., 106 Elias ave., Evansville, Ind.
Janssen, Recmt, Huron, Ohio.

Joerris, Peter, Poland, Clay Co., Ind.
Johnston, G. H., 2301 Green st., Phila., Pa.
Johnson, J. O., Schuyl. Haven, Schuyl. Co., Pa.
Johnston, Dr. T. S , Lebanon, Pa.
Judt, Fr., Louisville, Ky.

Kanne, A., Lacrosse, Wis.
Keener, H. F., Berlin, Somerset Co., Pa.
Kefauver, L. H., Tiffin, Ohio.
Kehm, Jacob, Sellersville, Bucks Co., Pa.
Keller, Christian, Dridesburg, Pa.
Keller, Christian F., Louisville, Ky.
Keller, Eli, Zionsville, Lehigh Co., Pa.
Keller, Henry, Boalsburg, Centre Co., Pa.
Keller, Joseph A., Bucyrus, Crawford Co., O.
Keller, Reuben, Erie, Monroe Co., Mich.
Kemm, L., Waukesba, Wis.
Kommerer, Dr., D., Wooster, Ohio.
Kendig, John M., Columbiana, Ohio.
Kercher, J., La Rose, Marshall Co., Pa.
Kern, A., Monticello, Jones Co., Iowa.
Kerschner, J. D., Millersburg, Dauphin Co., Pa.
Kerschner, J. B., Prof., Mac'sb'g, Frank. Co., Pa.
Kerschner, L. M., Greenville, Ohio.
Kessler, S. N. I., Mulberry, Clinton Co., Ind.
Kester, Joseph, Canaan, Wayne Co., Ohio.
Keyser, H. A., Mahanoy City, Schuylkill Co., Pa.
Kieffer, Harry M., Norristown, Pa.
Kieffer, John B., Prof., Lancaster, Pa.
Kieffer, J. Spangler, Hagerstown, Md.
Kieffer, Dr. M., Gettysburg, Pa.
King, Hiram, Bellefonte, Centre Co., Pa.
King, Henry, Baltimore, O.
Klar, J. C., Navarre, Stark Co., Ohio.
Klein, D. G., Walker, Centre Co., Pa.
Klein, J., Schuylkill Haven, Schuylkill Co., Pa.
Klein, Dr. H. J., Gallon, Crawford Co., Ohio.
Kline, Alpha K., Elderton, Armstrong Co., Pa.
Klingler, J., Stoutsville, Fairfield Co., O.
Klopp, Dr. D. E., 1541 N. 7th st., Philada., Pa.
Kluge, J. T., Sheboygan, Wis.
Knappenberger, J.W., Delmont, Westm'd Co., Pa.
Knepper, B., Wellersburg, Somerset Co., Pa.
Knepper, Chas., Mansfield Val., Alleg'y Co., Pa.
Knepper, Charles O., Tiffin, O.
Kols, J., Wheeling, Cook Co., Ill. -
Knierien, John, Parks Grove, St. Clair Co., Mo.
Knorst, J. D., 71 Locust st., Buffalo, N. Y.
Knipe, Jesse B., Chester Springs, Chester Co., Pa.
Kohl, Peter, Al, Fulton Co., Ohio.
Kohler, Pheon S., Egypt, Lehigh Co., Pa.
Kohler, W., Dahlgreen, Carver Co., Minn.
Kouatzgy, Augustus, Hammansburg, Ohio.
Koplin, A. D., Hellertown, Northampton Co., Pa.
Korthüer, Dr. D., Bucyrus, Crawford Co., O.
Krahn, Albert, Wabasha, Minn.
Krobs,W. E., Bloomsb'g, Columbia Co., Pa.
Kremer, Dr. A. H., Carlisle, Pa.
Kremer, A. R., Emmitsburg, Frederick Co., Md.
Kremer, Ellie N., Bedford, Pa.
Kremer, Dr. F.W., Lebanon, Pa.

Kramer, L. G., Hagerstown, Md.
Kretzing, John, Newport, Perry Co., Pa.
Kriste, Chas. U., Fort Wayne, Ind.
Kroh, Daniel, Erie, Mich.
Krüger, Julius H., San Francisco, Cal.
Kuckermann, F. W. H., New Knoxville, O.
Kuenzler, F., Waukesha, Wis.
Kuhl, I. G., Kelly's Island, O.
Kuhlen, G., Vermillion, Erie Co., Ohio.
Kuhn, Jacob, Millersburg, Iowa Co., Iowa.
Kuhn, Samuel, Hummelstown, Dauphin Co., Pa.
Kunz, Rudolph, Hazleton, Pa.
Kurtz, Dr. Henry, Franklin, Sheboygan Co., Wis.
Kurtz, Julius, Shamokin, Northumb'd Co., Pa.
Kurtzman, G., Sparta, Wis.   [ter, Pa.
Külling, Dr. John, 336 W. Chestnut st., Lancas-
Kützel, W., Lowell, Dodge Co., Wis.
Kuss, G., 41½ Sherman st., Buffalo, N. Y.

Lady, D. B., Manor Station, Westmorel'd Co., Pa.
Lake, Orange E., Walkersville, Fred'k Co., Md.
Landis, W. M., Reisersburg, Centre Co., Pa.
Lantz, Daniel, Freeston, Ill.
Lasure, L. B., Greensburg, Westmorel'd Co., Pa.
Leberman, D. D., Meadville, Crawford Co., Pa.
Leberman, J. J., Louisville, O.
Leberman, L. D., Pottstown, Montg'y Co., Pa.
Lefever, David P., Essex, Page Co., Iowa.
Lefever, J. M., Fairfield, Green Co., Ohio.
Lefever, Wm. D., Littlestown, Adams Co., Pa.
Leich, F. P., Rieuville, Wash. Co., Wis.
Leidy, Geo., Norristown, Montgomery Co., Pa.
Leinbach, A. S., Reading, Pa.
Leinbach, Dr. C. H., Stouchsburg, Berks Co., Pa.
Leinbach, J. Calvin, Stouchsburg, Berks Co., Pa.
Leinbach, S. A., Copley, Lehigh Co., Pa.
Leinbach, T. C., Womelsdorf, Berks Co., Pa.
Leinbach, J. H., Reading, Pa.
Leisse, Henry, Orwigsburg, Schuyl. Co., Pa.
Leisse, Aaron H., Host, Berks Co., Pa.
Leiter, Dr. S. R., Wadsworth, Medina Co., O.
Leonard, G. H., Basil, Fairfield Co., O.
Lerch, J. V., Ashland, Ohio.
Leutzinger, H., Sturgis, Mich.
Levan, P. K., Wilkesbarre, Luzerne Co., Pa.
Lichliter, W. F., Woodstock, Va.
Lienkemper, C., Waukon, Allamakee Co., Iowa.
Limberg, C. A., Butler, Butler Co., Pa.
Linderman, F. S., Blain, Perry Co., Pa.
Lisberger, R., Bath, Northampton Co., Pa.
Lohr, O. T., East India.
Long, H. F., Sarah, Blair Co., Pa.
Long, P. A., Taneytown, Md.
Long, Samuel C., Wilton, Muscatine, Co., Iowa.
Long, T., Salem, N. C.
Loos, L. K., Bethlehem, Pa.
Loos, N. H., Bellevue, Huron Co., Ohio.
Loose, J. S., Harrisonburg, Va.
Loucks, Michael, Somerset, Ohio.
Love, J. W., Greensburg, Pa.
Lukens, Charles, Frankford, Philadelphia Co., Pa.
Luscher, N., Triadelphia, W. Va.

Martin, Chas. T., Franklin, Sheboygan Co., Wis.
Martin, Dr. Geo. H., Woodstock, Va.
Massiaky, G. H., Wall Rose, Beaver Co., Pa.
Mase, Silas, Massillon, Ohio.
Matzinger, Isaac, Clay City, Clay Co., Ind.
Mauger, S. P., Canal Winchester, Ohio.
May, Josiah, Balm, Mercer Co., Pa.
Mayer, L. J., Boyertown, Berks Co., Pa.
McCaughey, Wm., Miamisburg, Mont. Co., O.
McCauley, Dr. C. F., Reading, Pa.
McConnell, J., Salina, Westmoreland Co., Pa.
Meas, Dr. Samuel, Cincinnati, Ohio.
Mechling, Geo. Z., Hamilton, Ohio.
Meckley, John, Petersburg, Mahoning Co., O.
Meese, David J., Sandusky, Ohio.
Metzger, D. F., Higginsville, Schuylkill Co., Pa.
Meyer, H. A., Watertown, Wis.
Merz, A., Berne, Dodge Co., Minn.
Michael, J., Winamac, Pulaski Co., Indiana.
Mickley, J. M., Newburg, Cumberland Co., Pa.
Miller, Abraham, Lake, Stark Co., Ohio.
Miller, E. D., Ringtown, Schuylkill Co., Pa.
Miller, Henry, Waynesboro', Franklin Co., Pa.
Miller, J. David, Martinsburg, Blair Co., Pa.
Miller, Dr. J. O., York, Pa.
Miller, M. A., Carrollton, Ohio.
Miller, Simon S., Boonsboro', Md.
Millett, J. K., McEwensville, Pa.
Mishler, Mahlon H., Weatherly, Carbon Co., Pa.
Mohr, F. J., Quakertown, Bucks Co., Pa.
Moore, Jarius P., Millersville, Lancaster Co., Pa.
Mosser, H., Reading, Pa.
Motter, Isaac M., Waynesboro', Franklin Co., Pa.
Mühlmeier, Dr. Henry A., Franklin, Sheboygan
     Co., Wis.
Mühlhaupt, J., Salem, Marion Co., Oregon.
Mull, George F., Lebanon, Pa.
Müller, E. L., Wheeling, Va.
Müller, H. F., Fort Wayne, Ind.
Müller, Martin, Fostoria, O.
Mutschler, C. H., Jonestown, Lebanon Co., Pa.
Myers, S. P., Anna, Union Co., Ill.

Neille, J., Lyons, Ill.
Nau, M., Mt. Eaton, Wayne Co., Ohio.
Neff, J. G., Shenandoah, Schuylkill Co., Pa.
Neihoff, John, Archbold, Fulton Co., Ohio.
Neuber, J. G., 1832 E. Montgomery st., Phila., Pa.
Nevin, Dr. J. W., Lancaster, Pa.
Nicolai, J. A., Abilene, Dickinson Co., Kan.
Noll, Moritz, Bellaire, Belmont Co., Ohio.
North, John M., Mercersburg, Pa.
Noss, John G., Westminster, Carroll Co., Md.
Novinger, J. A., New Bedford, Coshocton Co., O.

Oechsner, Chr., Norwood, Carver Co., Minn.
Oplinger, R. F., Edinburg, Ill.
Orth, Jacob, Yankton, Dakota.
Otting, E. H., Warren, Trumbull Co., O.

Pannabecker, J. H., Elizabethtown, Lancaster
     Co., Pa.
Peightal, Isaac N., Pattonsville, Bedford Co., Pa.

Pence, John, Fremont, Clarke Co., Ohio.
Pennypacker, J. J., Rimersburg, Pa.
Peters, M., Hamburg, Berks Co., Pa.
Peters, W. J., West Lodi, Ohio.
Peters, J. A., Lancaster, Pa.
Pilgram, Fred'k, Greenville, Mercer Co., Pa.
Poerner, J. D., Watertown, Wis.
Pontius, J. W., Cochranton, Crawford Co., Pa.
Porter, Dr. Thos. C., Prof., Easton, Pa.
Praßkachatis, L., Terre Haute, Ind.
Prugh, Peter C., Germantown, Ohio.

Rabauser, Reuben, Dallastown, York Co., Pa.
Ream, Solomon, Fulton, Mich.
Reber, J. Alvin, McConnelsburg, Fulton Co., Pa.
Reber, T. N., Macungie, Lehigh Co., Pa.
Reichard, Richard B., Springboro', Ohio.
Reichs, G. J., Rising Sun, Ind.
Reily, Prof. Wm. M., Meyers'n, Lebanon Co., Pa.
Reinecke, Dr. E. W., Nazareth, Pa.
Reiter, C. H., James Creek, Huntingdon Co., Pa.
Reiter, D. H., Berrien Spring, Berrien Co., Mich.
Reiter, Dr. I. H., Miamisburg, Ohio.
Renter, W., Monroeville, Ohio.
Rettig, George, Monticello, Iowa.
Rettig, John, Wheatland, Clinton Co., Iowa.
Richards, J., Fremont, Ohio.   [Kan-
Richards, Emanuel, Grand Prairie, Brown Co.
Richter, L., Ada, Hardin Co., O.
Riegel, Daniel, Dillsburg, York Co., Pa.
Ricke, Herman, Jeffersonville, Ind.
Rike, Levi, Farmersville, Ohio.
Rinker, H. St. John, Lovettsville, Loudon Co., Va.
Rittenhouse, C. A., Cherryville, Northampton
     Co., Pa.
Romeis, John, Van Dyne, Fon du Lac Co., Wis.
Rodenburg, F. W., Lanesville, Harrison Co., Ind.
Roeck, J., Ebenezer, Erie.
Roeder, Samuel M., Centre Hall, Centre Co., Pa.
Roentgen, J. H. C., Box 153, La Crosse, Wis.
Roesch, J. J., Titusville, Crawford Co., Pa.
Romich, A., Beaver Springs, Snyder Co., Pa.
Rossiter, Joel T., 208 N. Calvert st., Balt., Md.
Roth, Geo. W., Point Pleasant, Bucks Co., Pa.
Rothrock, D., Durham, Bucks Co., Pa.
Rowland, M. S., Spring City, Chester Co., Pa.
Ruetenik, Dr. H. J., 991 Scranton ave., Cleveland,
     Ohio.
Ruetenik, N., Higgin's Pt., Brown Co., Ohio.
Ruetenik, Paul J., Boeger's Store, Osage Co., Mo.
Ruhl, J. Frostburg, Md.
Ruhl, J. B., South West, Elkhart Co., Ind.
Ruhl, John G., Kenton, Hardin Co., Ohio.
Ruhl, P., Auburn, De Kalb Co., Ind.
Rupley, F. A., Martinsburg, Blair Co., Pa.
Rupp, Wm., Manchester, Carrol Co., Md.
Russell, Dr. Geo. B., Washington City, D. C.
Rust, Dr. H., Prof., Tiffin, Ohio.
Rusterholz, H., Bluffton, Allen Co., Ohio.

Sandos, H. H., Baltimore, Fairfield Co., Ohio.
Sandoe, W. B., Butler, Pa.
Sangree, M. H., Everett, Bedford Co., Pa.

Sachse, Dr. J. W., Cavetown, Wash. Co., Md.
Saal, G., 118 Forsyth st., Pittsburgh, Pa.
Saarber, Fred't J., York, Pa.
Schaad, Fred., Rogersville, Tuscarawas Co., O.
Schade, K. F. A., 523 Broadway, Cleveland, Ohio.
Schaaf, Chas., 53 W. Washington st., Ft. Wayne, Ind
Schaaf, Chas. M., Bristol, Morgan Co., Ohio.
Schaub, David, Hereford, Berks Co., Pa.
Schaeffer, Prof. N. C., Kutztown, Berks Co., Pa.
Schaeffer, W. C., Kutztown, Berks Co., Pa.
Schaffer, S. D., Milton, Northumberl'd Co., Pa.
Schatz, Jos. L., Randolph, Ohio.
Scheel, C., Plymouth, Ind.
Scheer, Geo. A., 2250 N. 5th st., Philadelphia, Pa.
Schick, John M., Orbisonia, Huntingdon Co., Pa.
Schick, G. B., Milltown, N. J.
Schiller, C., 30 Scott st., Toledo, Ohio.
Schlappig, Jos. H., Ravanna, Mercer Co., Mo.
Schmid, J. G.
Schneck, A., Norn, Jasper Co., Iowa.
Schoedler, D. E., Oley, Berks Co., Pa.
Schoepfle, Christ. H., Carothers, Seneca Co., O.
Schory, P. D., Lancaster, Ohio.
Schroth, Daniel, Marion, Ohio.
Schultz, C. W., Camden, N. J.
Schultz, James A., Reading, Pa.
Schwartz, F. H., Robesonia, Berks Co., Pa.
Schwartz, L. D., Boston, Mass.
Schwartz, P. A., Tamaqua, Schuylkill Co., Pa.
Schwoeder, F. R., Cumberland, Md.
Sechler, Jacob, Hanover, York Co., Pa.
Sechler, John M., Dice Bell, Mont. Co., Pa.
Sechler, Jos., Lena, Stephenson Co., Ill.
Seipel, H. F., Henrietta, Blair Co., Pa.
Seyring, A., Crothersville, Indiana.
Shade, J. S., Astoria, Ill.
Shaull, H., Tiffin, O.
Shaw, Samuel, Bloomville, Seneca Co., Ohio.
Shelp, L. C., Doylestown, Bucks Co., Pa.
Shenkle, A. B., Millersville, Lancaster Co., Pa.
Shepler, J. R., Nimisilla, Ohio.　[Co., Pa.
Shoemaker, D. O., Shamokin, Northumberland
Shoemaker, E. D., Bedford, Bedford Co., Pa.
Shoemaker, J. G., Aaronsburg, Centre Co., Pa.
Shouts, J. H., Baltimore, Md.
Shuey, D. B., New Providence, Lancaster Co., Pa.
Shumaker, Hiram, Lawrence, Kansas.
Shumaker, J. B., Lancaster, Pa.
Shuford, J. H., Hickory Tavern, N. C.
Shuford, M. L., Du-kittsville, Md.　[Co., Md.
Shulenberger, Anthony, Mt. Pleasant, Frederick
Shulenberger, W. C. D., St. Petersburg, Clarion
　Co., Pa.
Siegel, O. W. E., Scioto, Monroe Co., Pa.
Siles, Isaac A., Dakota, Ill.
Skinner, J. B., Pulaski, Williams Co., Ohio.
Skyles, N. H., Jefferson, Frederick Co., Md.
Smith, J. E., Dath, Northampton Co., Pa.
Smith, G. Wm. H., Xenia, Green Co., O.
Smith, J. A., Anamosa, Jones Co., Iowa.
Smith, M. A., Nazareth, Northampton Co., Pa.

Smith, R. H., York, Pa.
Snyder, G. W., Harrisburg, Pa.
Snyder, J. F., Manor Dale, Westmoreland Co., Pa.
Snyder, N. Z., S. Bethlehem, Northampton Co., Pa.
Snyder, W. H. H., Harrisburg, Pa.
Souder, J. Mortimer, Wilhelmsburg, Alleg'y Co., Pa.
Sorber, Geo. S., Vincent, Chester Co., Pa.
Sorber, William, Vincent, Chester Co., Pa.
Spangler, Aaron, York, Pa.
Spangler, E., Edgarton, Williams Co., O.
Spangler, H. T., Lancaster, Fairfield Co., O.
Spangler, P. J., Farmer Centre, Ohio.
Spies, Wm., Decatur, Adams Co., Ind.
Stahr, John S., Prof., Lancaster, Pa.
Stahr, Isaac F., Lock Haven, Clinton Co., Pa.
Staley, Dr. G. L., Knoxville, Frederick Co., Md.
Stambaugh, Levi D., Smith's Station, York Co., Pa.
Stauffer, A. S., Lykens, Dauphin Co., Pa.
Stauffer, T. F., Butler, Butler Co., Pa.
Stechow, William, Beaverton, Pike Co., O.
Steckel, L. D., Dale City, Somerset Co., Pa.
Steele, James, West Brookfield, Ohio.
Stein, J. P., Pottsville, Pa.
Steiner, J., Greenville, Ohio.
Steinmetz, John W., Reading, Pa.
Stem, T. O., Easton, Northampton Co., Pa.
Stepler, John H., Lima, Ohio.
Stern, Herman J., Louisville, Ky.
Stein, M. G. L., 30 Chatham St., Indianapolis, Ind.
Stewart, W. I., St. Thomas, Franklin Co., Pa.
Steinacker, W. W., Dale, Outagamie Co., Wis.
Stoner, John S., Navarre, Stark Co., Ohio.
Stoner, A. B., Norristown, Pa.
Strassburger, M. S., Allentown, Pa.
Straemer, F., Orrville, Wayne Co., Ohio.
Stuck, J., Hillgrove, Ohio.
Stump, Fred. W., Orangeville, Ill.
Super, Dr. H. W., Prof., Collegeville, Montgomery
　Co., Pa.
Swander, J. I., Latrobe, Westmoreland Co., Pa.
Sweitzer, S., Lincoln, Lancaster Co., Pa.
Sykes, John H., Greencastle, Franklin Co., Pa.

Tallheim, Henry, Edenburg, Shenandoah Co. Va.
Taylor, Daniel R., Northampton, Ohio.
Teudick, P., Tiffin, Seneca Co., Ohio.
Terborg, J. E., 495 4th St., Milwaukee, Wis.
Thomas, B., Malvern, Carroll Co., Ohio.
Thompson, Jos. B., Shannondale, Clarion Co., Pa.
Titzel, J. H., Irwin, Westmoreland Co., Pa.
Tobias, D. C., Lititz, Lancaster Co., Pa.
Toensmeier, Aug., Ironton, Lawrence Co., O.
Transue, S., Kutztown, Pa.
Trautman, H., 19 Louis St., Cleveland, Ohio.
Trexler, Peter M., Salisbury, Rowan Co., N. C.
Trieber, M., Sandusky, Ohio.
Truxal, Albert E., Somerset, Pa.

Vanderaloot, F. E., Herndon, Fairfax Co., Va.
Vanderaloot, J. Samuel, 4042 Haverford St., Phila.
Van Hoagan, John, Collegeville, Mont. Co., Pa.
Van Horne, Dr. D., 647 Marshall St., Phila., Pa.
Vitz, P., Lafayette, Ind.

Voegelin, John, Dunkirk, N. Y.
Vogt, John, Delaware, Ohio.
Vriesen, D. W., Johnsonville, Sheboygan Co., Wis.
Wagner, S. G., Allentown, Pa.
Wagner, S. T., Landisburg, Pa.
Wahl, F., Bluffton, Wells Co., Ind.
Waldecker, G. F., Lima, Allen Co., Ohio.
Walk, Frederick, Philadelphia, Pa.
Wanner, Aaron, York, Pa.
Warren, B., Deckert, Franklin Co., Tenn.
Wassich, W., Pulaski, Williams Co., Ohio.
Weaver, J., Sidney, Ohio.
Weaver, R. C., Cooperstown, Lehigh Co., Pa.
Weber, Geo., Blairstown, Benton Co., Iowa.
Wegert, Henry, Haskins, Wood Co., Ohio.
Weidner, U. H., Chalfant, Bucks Co., Pa.
Weiser, Dr. C. Z., East Greenville, Mont. Co., Pa.
Weiss, Benjamin, Leubartsville, Berks Co., Pa.
Weiss, Dr. J., Bucyrus, Ohio.
Weiss, Dr. L. S., York, Pa.
Welker, Dr. G. W., Greensboro', Guilf'd Co., N. C.
Welker, H. J., Coopersburg, Lehigh Co., Pa.
Wernly, J., Freeport, Ill.
Wettach, E. D., Sulphur Springs, Crawford Co., O
Whitmer, A. C., Altoona, Blair Co., Pa.
Whitmore, A. J., Middlebrook, Augusta Co., Va.
Whitmore, D. M., Charlesville, Bedford Co., Pa.
Wiant, Jacob F., Lancaster, Pa.
Wiehle, Dr. J. G., 607 Fairmount av., Philada., Pa.
Wiers, N., New Bavaria, Henry Co., Ohio.
Willers, Dr. D., Fayette, Seneca Co., N. Y.
Williams, B. Garver, Coderus, York Co., Pa.
Williard, E. R., White Pigeon, Mich.
Williard, Dr. G. W., Tiffin, Ohio.
Winter, John, Crestline, Ohio.
Winters, Dr. David, Dayton, Ohio.
Winters, T. H., Xenia, Green Co., Ohio.
Wisner, Christian, Upper Sandusky, Ohio.
Wissler, H., Mechanicstown, Frederick Co., Md.
Wittenweiler, W., Rogersville, Tuscarawas Co., O.
Witthoff, F. G., Homeworth, Columbiana Co., O.
Woehler, B. Th., Appleton, Wis.
Wolbach, John, Troutville, Clearfield Co., Pa.
Wolff, D. M., Prof., Penn Hall, Centre Co., Pa.
Wolff, Dr. G., Myerstown, Lebanon Co., Pa.
Wolff, D. U., Myrrstown, Lebanon Co., Pa.
Wolff, Simon, Lewisburg, Union Co., Pa.

Xanders, Wm. H., Easton, Pa.

Yearick, W. R., Hilltown, Bucks Co., Pa.
Yearick, Z. A., Turbotsv'e, Northumberl'd Co., Pa.
Yockey, S. B., Xenia, Ohio.
Yost, F. C., Thornville, Ohio.
Young, J. Chr., 33 Henry St., Cleveland, Ohio.
Young, J. E., Conesville, Muscatine Co., Iowa.

Zacharias, George M., Harrisburg, Pa.
Zacharias, G. H., Up. Strasburg, Franklin Co., Pa.
Zahner, Dr. J. G., Shanesv'e, Tuscarawas Co., O.
Zartman, Allen H., Helena, Ohio.
Zehring, J. D., Coderus, York Co., Pa.
Zeller, M. F., Allentown, Pa.
Zenke, Ludwig, Kiel, Manitowoc Co., Wis.
Zerbe, Prof. Alvin S., Collegeville, Montgomery
　Co., Pa.
Zieber, Dr. W. K., Hanover, York Co., Pa.
Ziegler, A. F., Bingen, Northampton Co., Pa.
Ziegler, W. H., Goshen, Indiana.
Ziegler, G., Paris, Stark Co., Ohio.
Ziegler, J., York, Pa.
Ziegler, Jacob, Castle, Andre Co., Mo.
Ziegler, L., Bongards, Carver Co., Minn.
Zimmerman, C. D., Galion, Crawford Co., Ohio.
Zinck, H. K., Stone Creek, Tuscarawas Co., O.
Zinzler, George, Newtonsb'g, Manitowoc Co., Wis.
Zinkhan, L. F., Manheim, Lancaster Co., Pa.
Zipf, C. G., 194 Aaron St., Cleveland, Ohio.
Zumpe, G. P., Terre Haute, Vigo Co., Ind.
Zumpe, J. B., Canfield, Mahoning Co., Ohio.

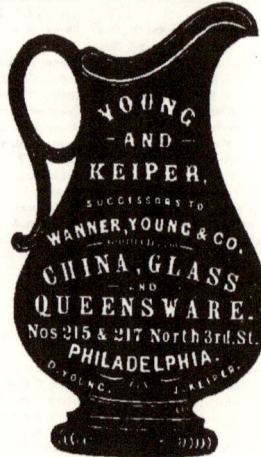

www.ingramcontent.com/pod-product-compliance
Lightning Source LLC
Chambersburg PA
CBHW021446090426
42739CB00009B/1663